George Washington

REMEMBERS

George Washington, 1772, by Charles Willson Peale. Unaware of another military career just a few years away, 40-year-old George Washington (1732– 1799) chose his old French and Indian War uniform for his first portrait. The painting evokes young Washington's wilderness experiences, which prepared him for a central role in later events. *(Washington and Lee University, Lexington, Virginia)*

George Washington

REMEMBERS

*Reflections on the
French and
Indian War*

Edited by Fred Anderson

With contributions by
Philander D. Chase
Don Higginbotham
Burton K. Kummerow
Christine Smith
Martin West
Rosemarie Zagarri

ROWMAN & LITTLEFIELD PUBLISHERS, INC.
Lanham Boulder New York Toronto Oxford

ROWMAN & LITTLEFIELD PUBLISHERS, INC.

Published in the United States of America by Rowman & Littlefield Publishers, Inc.
A wholly owned subsidary of The Rowman & Littlefield Publishing Group, Inc.
4501 Forbes Boulevard, Suite 200, Lanham, Maryland 20706
www.rowmanlittlefield.com

PO Box 317
Oxford
OX2 9RU, UK

THIS PUBLICATION HAS BEEN MADE POSSIBLE IN PART BY THE GENEROUS
SUPPORT OF THE McCUNE FOUNDATION.

The generous help and support of Philander D. Chase and Beverly H. Runge of The Papers
of George Washington at the University of Virginia is gratefully acknowledged.

British Library Cataloguing in Publication Information Available

Library of Congress Cataloging-in-Publication Data
    Washington, George, 1732-1799.
    [Remarks]
    George Washington remembers : reflections on the French and Indian War / edited by
Fred Anderson.
        p.   cm.
    Includes bibliographical references (p.   ) and index.
    ISBN 0-7425-3372-7 (hardcover : alk. paper) ; ISBN 0-7425-3506-1 (deluxe)
    1. Washington, George, 1732–1799. 2. United States—History—French and Indian War,
1755–1763. I. Anderson, Fred, 1949– II. Title.
    E312.23.W35 2004
    940.2'534—dc22
                                                                            2003021103

Printed in the United States of America

∞ The paper used in this publication meets the minimum requirements of American
National Standard for Information Sciences—Permanence of Paper for Printed Library
Materials, ANSI/NISO Z39.48-1992.

Contents

Contents

Fred Anderson
University of Colorado, Boulder

Foreword

ALTHOUGH individual historical documents have occasionally become the subject of whole books—the Declaration of Independence and the Gettysburg Address come to mind—it is relatively rare for such a thing to happen. It may therefore be worthwhile to explain how this volume, which focuses on the only piece of autobiographical writing George Washington ever did, came to be. It is in fact just one aspect of a multidimensional public effort, based in Pittsburgh, to commemorate the 250th anniversary of the French and Indian War.

In 1999 the directors of several French and Indian War–era historic sites in western Pennsylvania—Jumonville Glen/Fort Necessity, National Battlefield, Braddock's Field, Dunbar's Camp, Kittanning, Fort Pitt/Point State Park, Fort Ligonier, and Bushy Run Battlefield—began coordinating their site interpretations and outreach programs in preparation for the 250th anniversary of the French and Indian War. Later, under the sponsorship of a nonprofit agency, the Allegheny Conference on Community Development, and with the help of that organization's senior vice-president, Laura Fisher, this alliance expanded to include additional sites and organizations in the region. The goal was to build public awareness of an event that influenced the history of the United States (and indeed the world) more decisively than most modern Americans realize. In so doing, participants in the commemorative effort hoped to conserve and make accessible the physical legacies of our common past.

Winston Churchill once called the Seven Years' War—the larger conflagration of which the French and Indian War was the North American phase—the first world war. He had good reason to do so: the antagonists—France, Austria, Russia and Spain on one side, Britain and Prussia on the other—fought land battles in Europe, North America, the Caribbean, West Africa, India, and the Philippines, and naval engagements on the North Atlantic, the Mediterranean, and the Indian Ocean. This great struggle (referred to as both the Seven Years' War and the French and Indian War in this volume), ended in a victory of unprecedented scope and decisiveness for Great Britain. That victory, ironically, helped foster the American Revolution that followed, just a little over a decade later. It is altogether appropriate that an organization based in Pittsburgh should take the lead in commemorating the conflict, for it grew out of clashes between France and Britain over control of the Forks of the Ohio River—the confluence of the Allegheny and Monongahela, where the city now stands. Both powers quite accurately understood that spot as the key to controlling the North American interior, and hence the future of the continent.

It is also fitting that this particular document should have a prominent part in the commemoration, for George Washington played a central (if unintentional) role in starting the war in 1754. In the following year he served in General Edward Braddock's ill-fated expedition against the French at the Forks, then led Virginia's troops in the effort to defend the colonial frontier in 1756 and 1757, and finally participated in the campaign by which the British took control of Fort Duquesne and the upper Ohio in 1758. There is no more surprising development in U.S. history than that this loyal servant of the British crown, less than two decades later, should have agreed to lead the military struggle for American independence as commander-in-chief of the Continental Army.

The events of the frontier war that shaped his life as a young man were principally what George Washington remembered when he wrote the autobiographical "Remarks" that are here reproduced, transcribed, annotated, commented upon, and explained. This extremely private document—which Washington intended only for the eyes of his biographer, David Humphreys, and which he instructed Humphreys to burn after reading—was purchased for the 250th anniversary observances with funds generously made available by the Laurel Foundation, Suzy and Jim Broadhurst, and Diane and Glen Meakem. During the commemoration it will be placed on public display for the first time; thereafter it will remain permanently in western Pennsylvania, the scene of so many of the events its author describes.

The part that this volume plays in the larger commemorative scheme is to allow ordinary citizens to inspect and reflect on a document of great significance, which for more than two centuries has been accessible only to its owners and a tiny number of scholars. The George Washington who reveals himself in this vivid, little-known text is both less familiar and far more intriguing than the half-mythological figure whose face we see daily on the dollar bill. Readers will find this Washington as willing to reminisce about his war experiences as any veteran, and as subject to the emotions of ambition, pride, and fear as we are, ourselves.

Undoubtedly a great deal more will come of the 250th anniversary of the French and Indian War than the opportunity to discover these personal dimensions of the man who contributed more to the beginnings of the United States than any other. Yet even if, somehow, nothing more came of the whole commemoration than the chance to understand George Washington a little better—the opportunity this document affords to imagine him as a human being, rather than to take him for granted as a monument—that alone would be sufficient.

Philander D. Chase
Editor in Chief,
The Papers of George
Washington

Introduction

S ELDOM does a historical document—particularly one written by a person with no literary pretensions whatsoever—merit a book of its own. The ten-and-a-half-page autobiographical "Remarks" that George Washington wrote about his early life, when he was in his midfifties, is such a document, because it gives us the rarest of glimpses into the psyche of this most essential but most emotionally remote of the founding fathers—a man, who, in spite of or perhaps because of the great fame that he so eagerly sought and achieved, has remained something of an enigma even to his countrymen—a seemingly unapproachable figure hidden behind his own silences and the monumental myth that surrounds him. Everyone knows Washington or at least is familiar with his image, which Americans see daily on their currency, but we struggle when we try to imagine him as a real person with frustrated ambitions, personal anxieties, and feelings of guilt, as well as a keen sense of humor and a zest for life's pleasures.

Unlike Winston Churchill, who said that he knew what history would say about him because he intended to write that history—and did so—Washington was content to preserve his papers and let future historians make of them what they would. He also was unlike most of the other founding fathers in steadfastly refusing to write any sort of autobiography or memoirs with the single exception of the "Remarks," a very private piece of writing, which he intended only for the eyes of his trusted friend and would-be biographer, David Humphreys, and which survived only because Humphreys neglected to follow Washington's explicit instructions to destroy or return the document once he had extracted from it the information that he required.

Washington's lack of literary pretensions aside, he proves in the "Remarks" to be a compelling storyteller, specifically a teller of French and Indian War stories that are both honest and very human—stories that obviously had deep personal meaning for Washington. Accessible as Washington is in these pages, readers will be greatly aided by the factual background information found in Martin West's annotation. Their understanding of both Washington and his "Remarks" will be further enhanced by their reading of the three thoughtful essays included in this volume. Rosemarie Zagarri puts the "Remarks" in the context of Humphreys' never fully realized biography project. Fred Anderson puts the document in the context of the anxious time during which Washington wrote it, the years 1787–1788 when the Constitution was being written and ratified and Washington faced the personally troubling question of whether or not to accept the presidency. Don Higginbotham puts the "Remarks" in the context of Washington's ardent youthful ambitions and the high degree of personal visibility which his French and Indian War exploits brought him both within and outside Virginia.

Although this volume exposes some personal vulnerabilities in Washington, which he undoubtedly would have wished not to be exposed so publicly, it confirms in new ways what we always have known about Washington: that he was a man of exceptional integrity, courage, and good judgment. It also reveals Washington as a man who remembered his youthful experiences and came to terms with them in such a way as to enable him to move forward in the face of formidable difficulties to accomplish important new achievements for the nation to which he had so unalterably committed himself.

Note to the

Reader

WHAT follows is a facsimile of the 1787–1788 "Remarks" manuscript. After the facsimile is a new transcription of the document, prepared by the staff of The Papers of George Washington at the University of Virginia. In the transcription of the "Remarks," square brackets, [ ], indicate editorial insertions and angle brackets, < >, are used for text that is mutilated or illegible in the manuscript. Extensive notes by Fort Ligonier Director Martin West provide a context for Washington's comments.

The "Remarks" are Washington's unedited private thoughts, not intended for public consumption. In them, he comments on a draft biography prepared by his close friend, David Humphreys. Thus, readers will find three voices in the text: Colonel Humphreys's biographical passages, which appear as italics in the notes, General Washington's comments on the Humphreys text, and Martin West's end notes.

To explore the manuscript, you may want to first read the transcript, referring to the end notes for more background on the many people, places, and events mentioned in the text. Then, when you read George Washington's original words, you will better understand what he meant when he put quill to paper.

Part I

Page 1.ᵗ   Remarks

(1). It was the wish of my eldest brother (on whom the general concerns of the family devolved) that this was contemplated — My father died when I was only 10 years old.

(2). He was not appointed Adjutant General of the Militia of Virginia until after his return from the expedition to Carthagena. — Nor did he command the Colonial troops as that officer — These were under the Orders of Lⁱ Wᵐ Gooch Lt. Govⁱ of Virginia. He was the Senior in this of those which were raised in this Colony wᶜʰ, with those of the other Colonies, formed what was called the American Brigade — under Sir William Gooch — he was scarcely of age when he wrote this

(3) And from whom he had received many distinguished marks of patronage & favor

(4). His also — for the second Son (Augustine) left many children who are now living and inherit a very large portion of his Fathers Estate — perhaps the best part

Page. 2

(1) Before he was 20 years of age.

(2) He was then more than 21 years — as will appear from dates.

Page. 3

(1) At a most inclement Season, for he travelled over the Apalacheon Mountains, and passed through an uninhabited Country (except by a few tribes of Indians settled on the Banks of the Ohio) to Presque Isle, in the depth of winter, when the face of the Earth was covered with snow and the waters covered with Ice; the dist. from Wⁱˡˡˢᵇᵘʳᵍ to the then seat of Governⁱ at least 500 miles —

(2) It was on this occasion he was named by the half-King (as he was called) and the tribes of Nations with whom he treated Caunotaucarius (in English) the Town taker, which name being communicated to the nations of Indians, has been remembered by them ever since in all their transactions with him during the late war. —

Page 4.ᵗʰ

(1). This is a task to which G.W. feels himself very incompetent (with any degree of accuracy) from the badness of his memory — loss of Papers — mutilated state, in which those of that date were preserved — and the derangement of them by frequent removals, in the late war & want of time to collect and methodize them since. — However by the indefatigable Industry of the L's ⁱⁱ and the officers who serv...

ded his measures the Regiment was in great forwardness, at Alexandria (the general tendered early in the year 1754 want, and without waiting till the whole should be compleated—or for a detachment from the Independant Companies of the Southern Provinces (which had been ordered to the security required upon his service) or for troops which were raising in North Carolina and destined since in conjunction to oppose the incroachments of the French on our Western frontiers—He began his March in the Month of May in order to open the Road, and this he had to do almost the whole distance from Winchester, in the County of Frederick, yet more than 80 miles from Alexandria—from deposits—do.a—and for the especial purpose of seizing, if possible, before the French sd. arrive at it, the important Post at the conflux of the Alligany and Monongahela; with the advantages of which he was intimately acquainted the preceding year, and earnestly advised the securing of with Militia or some other temporary force—But notwithstanding all his exertions, the New, and uncommon difficulties he had to encounter, made more intolerable by incessant Rains and swelled waters of which he had many to cross, he had ascended the Laurel hill within 50 ms. short of his object when on the 9th of 30th he received intelligence from his scouts that the French had in force, siezed the Post he was pushing to obtain; having descended from Presque Isle by the River Le beauf and Alligany to this place—The object of his precipitate advance being thus defeated—the detachmt. which had arrived at Alexa. by water) around his Mr. being far in his rear and no acct. of the troops from No. Carolina. It was thought advisable to fall back a few miles, to a place known by the name of the great Meadows—abounding in forage more convenient for the purpose of forming a Magazine & bringing up the rear—and to advance (if we should ever be in force to do it) to the attack of the Post which the enemy now occupied and had called DuQuesne—At this place, some days after, we were joined by the above detachment of Regulars, consisting (before they were reduced on the March by desertion

desertion, sickness &c) of a Capt. McKay (a brave & worthy officer)—three Subalterns, and 100 Rank & file.—But previous to this junction the French sent a detachment to reconnoitre our line to obtain intelligence of our strength & position; notice of which being [given] by the Scouts, [G. W.] marched at the head of a party, attacked, killed 9, or 10, & captured 20 odd.— This, as soon as the enemy had assembled their Indian allies, brought their whole force upon us, consisting according to their own [account] compared with the resources that could be obtained, of about 1500 Men—His [consisting] of the detachment above mentioned, and between two & 300 warriors; for the few Indians which till then had attended [us] and who by reconnoitering the enemy in their march had got terrified at their number and resolved ~~...~~ had left us previous to the attack.— about 9 o'clock on the 3d of July the Enemy advanced with shouts, & dismal Indian yells to our Intrenchments, but was opposed by so warm, spirited, & constant a fire that to force the work in that way was abandoned. they then, from every little rising—tree—stump—stone—and bush kept up a constant galding fire upon us; which was returned in the best manner we could ~~...~~ till late in the afternoon. When their fell the most tremendous rain that can be conceived—filled our trenches with water—wet, not only the ammunition in the [French] boxes, and firelocks, but that ~~...~~ which was in a [temporary] stockade in the middle of the Intrenchment, erected for the ... purpose of its security, and that of the few there, we had, and left us nothing ... a few ... were ... provided with them) Bayonets for defence.— In this situation terms of capitulation were offered to us, which ... were the more readily acceded to, as we had no salt provisions, & but indifferently supplied with fresh; which, from the heat of the weather, would not keep, and because a full third of our number ... were, by this time, killed or wounded— The next morning we marched out with the honors of war, but were soon

plunder[ed]

* but which was impracticable without abandoning our stores &c. at the [hazard] ... which had brought us to this place had retained for provision[s]

contrary to the articles of capitulation deprived of great part of our Baggage by the Savages. — Our sick and wounded were left with a detachment under the care, and command of the worthy Doctr. Craik (for he was not only Surgeon to the Regiment but a Lieut. therein) and the remains of the Regim.t; and the detachment of Regulars, took up their line for the interior Country. — And at Winchester met two Companies from N.° Carolina on their march to join them — These being fresh, & properly provided, were ordered to proceed to Wills Creek or the block (since called Fort Cumberland) house for the purpose of covering the Frontiers. Where they were joined by a Company from Maryland, which about this time had been raised. — Cap.n McKay with his detachment remained at Winchester; — & the Virginia Regiment proceeded to Alexandria in order to recruit, & get supplied with cloathing & other necessarys of which they stood much in need. In this manner the winter was spent employed, when advice was received of the force destined for this Service, and the arrival of Sir Jn.° St. Clair, with some new arrangement of Rank by which no Officer who did not immediately derive his Com.n from the King could command one who did — This was too degrading for G.W. to submit to; accordingly, he resigned his Military employment; determining to serve the next campaign as a Volunteer; but, upon the arrival of Gen.l Braddock he was very particularly noticed by that General, — taken into his family as an extra: Aid — offered a Capt.n Com.n by brevet (which was the highest grade he had it in his power to bestow) and had, by the compliment of several blank Ensigncies given him to dispose of to the young Gentlemen of his acquaintance to supply the vacancies in the 44. and 48. Reg.ts which had arrived from Ireland.

In this capacity, he commenced his second Campaign; and used every proper opportunity, until it was too late & discipline had taken too deep root, to impress the Gen.l & the principal Officers around him, with the necessity of opposing the nature of his defence, to the mode of attack which, more than probable he would experience from the Canadian French and their Indians on his march, but so prepossessed were they in favr. of regularity & discipline and in such absolute contempt were these people held, that the admonition was suggested in vain. —

About the middle of June, this Armament consisting of the two Regiments from Ireland, some Independent companies and the Provincial troops of Virg.ª Mary.ᵈ & North Carolina, began to move from Fort Cumberland at which they had assembled — after several days March, and difficulties to which they had never been accustomed in Europ.ᵃ Car Service, in Champaign Countries. and of w.ᶜʰ they seemed to have had very little idea — the Gen.ˡ resolved to divide his force, and at the head of the first which was composed of &c. advanced, and committed the latter cover of his stores to advance, and commd. Dunbar with the second & the heavy Baggage & stores, to follow after. — By so doing, the first division approached the Monongahela the 8.ᵗʰ of July; at which time having so far recovered from a severe fever and delirium, from which he had been rescued by James's powder administered by the positive order of the Gen.ˡ as to travel in a covered Waggon, he Joined the first division and the next day tho' much reduced and very weak mounted his horse on cushions, & attended as one of his aids. —

About 10 Oclock on the 9.ᵗʰ, after the Van had crossed the Monongahela the Second time; to avoid an ugly defile (the season being very dry & waters low) and the rear yet in the River the Van was attacked and by the usual Hallooing and Whooping of the enemy, whom they could not see, were so disconcerted and confused as soon to fall into irretrievable disorder — The rear was forced forward to support them, but seeing no enemy, and themselves fasting every moment from the fire, a general panic having seized the troops took place, from which no exertions of the Officers could recover them — In the early part of the action some of the Irregulars (as they were called) without direct advanced to the right in loose order to attack it but this, unhappily from the unusual appearance of the movement being mistaken for Cowar & and running away, was discountenanced — and before it was too late, & the confusion became general an offer was made by G. W. to head the Provincials, & engage the enemy in their own way, but the impropriety of it was not seen into until it was too late for execution.

After this, many attempts were made to dislodge the enemy from an eminence on the Right but

they all proved ineffectual; and fatal to the Officers,
Who by great exertion, and example, endeavoured to
accomplish it — In one of these the Gen.ᵐ rec.ᵈ th wᵈ of
which he died; but previous to it, h'ad several horses
killed, & disabled under him — Capt.ⁿˢ Orme & Mor:
ris his two Aids de Camp, having received wounds which rendered them unable to attend.
G.W. remained the sole Aid through the day, to
the Gen; he also had one horse killed, and two
wounded under him — A ball through his hat —
and several through his clothes, but escaped un:
hurt — Sir Peter Halket (see.ᵈ in command) being
early killed — Lieut. Cor.ᵒ Burton & Sir Jn.ᵒ St. Clair (who
had the Rank of L.ᵗ Cor.ᵒ in the army) being bad:
ly wounded — Lieut.ᵗ Cor.ᵒ Gage (afterwards Gen.ᵉˡ
Gage) having rec.ᵈ a contusion — No person knew
in the disorder how things were
who the Surviving Sen.ᵗ Officer was.
& the Troop, by degrees going off in confusion;
without a ray of hope left, of further opposition
from those, G.W. placed the Gen.ᵐ placed in a small
covered Cart, which carried some of his most
essential equipage; and in the best order he
could, with the Troop (who were continued to be
fired at) brought him over the first ford of
the Monongahela; where they were
formed in the best order circumstances would
admit on a piece of rising ground; after wᶜʰ,
by the Gen.ᵐˢ order, he rode
forward to halt those which
had been earlier in the Retreat. Accordingly,
after crossing the Monongahela the second
time and ascending the heights, he found Lieut.ᵗ
Cor.ᵒ Gage, to whom he delivered the order and
then re:
turned to report his situation to the Gen.ᵐ by whom he was again re:
quested by the Gen.ᵐ whom he left
coming on, in his litter with the first halted
troops, to proceed (it then being after sundown)
to the second division under the command of
Cor.ᵒ Dunbar, to make arrangements for co:
vering the Retreat, and forwarding on provisions,
& refreshment, to the Retreating & wounded
Soldiery — To accomplish this (for the 2.ᵈ divis:
on was 40 odd miles in the Rear) it took up the whole
night

night & part of the next morning — which from
the weak state in which he was, and the fatigue,
and anxiety of the last 24 hours, rendered him in a
manner wholly unfit for the execution of the duty
he was sent upon — to the best of his power, however, he discharged it, and remained with the 2d.
division till the other joined it. — The shocking *

Happy was it for him, and the remains [of]
the first division that they left such a quantity
of valuable and enticing baggage on the field;
to occasion a scramble and contention
in the _____ of it among the enemy
for had _____
_____ which we avoided; and get cle[ar]
our rear, the whole except a few woodmen,
should have fallen. Of about 12 or hundred
which were in this action eight or g[?]
were killed or wounded, a men among them
brave & valuable Officers _____ — consequence of opposing compact bodies to the
sparse manner of Indian fighting, in woods, which
had been predicted, was now clearly verified that
_____ henceforward another mode obtained.

As soon as the two divisions, united, the
whole retreated towards Fort Cumberland, and
at an Incampment near the Great Meadows the
brave but unfortunate Genl. Braddock breathed
his last. — He was interred with the honors of
War and as it was left to GW [to] see this performed, & to mark out the spot for the reception of
his remains — to guard against a savage triumph,
if the place should be discovered — they were deposited in the _____ the Road over which the
army waggons &c. passed to hide every trace
by which the encampment could be discovered * — After this
event, the troops continued their march for, &
arriving at Fort Cumberland without molestation, and resolved to proceed to Philadelphia, by which means the frontiers of that State
but more especially those of Virginia and Maryland were laid entirely open by the van ano
_____ had prepared. — Of the dire-
ful consequence of this, GW, in a visit w[hich]
he immediately made to _____ per
_____ brought the Govr. & Council of Virg.
acquainted — Tho' in vain; they remonstrate against
the march of the B. Troops, to that place — then
proceeded to augment their own, the command of
wh[ich]

which under a very ~~enlarged & dignified~~ commission to
command all the troops now raised, or to be raised in the Colony, was given to him with very
extensive powers, and blank commissions to
~~appoint~~ all new officers. ~~appoint~~

About this time also, ~~about this time~~ all the
~~clamours~~ the discontents and clamours of
the Provincial officers, and the remonstrance
of ~~Colonel~~ G.W. in person, to Sir W. Shirley, the
then Com.r in chief of the British Forces in America; and, through the Sir W.'s Council to the King's
ministers ~~achieved establishment~~ with respect
to the ~~degradation~~ situation in which they were
placed a new ~~arrangement~~ took place by
the King's order, by which a ~~Provincial~~ officer was
to rank according to the Com.r he bore, but not
to those of the same grade on the established
Corps.—

As G.W. foresaw, so it happened, the frontiers were continually harassed ~~but not~~ having
force enough to carry the war to the gates of
Du Quesne, he could do no more than distribute
the troops along the frontier, in ~~stockaded~~
forts, more ~~with~~ a view to quiet the fears ~~of the inhabitants~~
from many expectation ~~of giving security to so~~
extensive a line, ~~never ceasing, in the mean~~
time in his attempt, to demonstrate to ~~all~~
~~to~~ Lord Loudoun—&c— that the only means
of preventing the devastations to which the
Middle States were exposed, was to remove the
cause. But matters in this time ~~were not~~
~~another quarter of the Continent~~ all applications were
unheeded till the year 1758 when an Expedition
against Fort Du Quesne was undertaken under the conduct of Gen.l Forbes, who tho' a brave
& good officer, was so much debilitated by bad
health, and so illy supplied with the means to carry on the expedition, that it was November before
the troops got to Loyalhannon; ~~there was~~
a the very point of abandoning the expedition,
when some supplies arriving, the Army took
up its March and moved forward, the Brigade
commanded by G.W. being the leading one.—

Previous to this, and during the time
the Army lay at Loyalhannon, the enemy sent
out a large detachment to reconnoitre our
camp, and to ascertain our strength, in consequence of Intelligence that they were within
2 Miles of the camp, a party commanded by Lt.
Col.o Mercer (a gallant & good officer,) was

sent to dislodge them between whom a severe conflict & her firing seemed which appearing to approach the camp it was conceived that our party was yielding the ground upon which 5th with permission of the Genl called for volunteers, and immediately marched at their head to sustain as was conjectured the retiring troops—Led by the firing till he came within or less than half a mile, & then ceasing, he detached Scouts to investigate the cause & communicate his approach to his friends (if any) advancing slowly in the mean time—But it being near dusk and the intelligence not having been fully disseminated among Genl Mercer's Corps, and they taking us for the enemy who had retreated approaching in another direction commenced a heavy fire upon the party which drew fire in return in spite of all the exertions of the officers one of whom & several privates were killed and many wounded before a stop could be put to it. To accomplish which 5th never was in more imminent danger by being between two fires, knocking up with his sword the presented pieces.

When the army had gotten within 12 or 15 miles of the Fort the enemy dispairing of its defence, blew it up—crossed the & Troops—and retreated by water to their settlements below.—Thus ended that campaign a little before Christmas in a very inclement weather and the last made during that War. 5th health by this time (case) had been declining for was by an inveterate disorder in his bowels) became so precarious, as to induce him (having soon quiet retired by this event to his country which was the principal inducement to his taking arms) to resign his Military appointment.—The solicitation of the Troops which he commanded to continue—their affect[d] farewell address to him when they found the situation of his health and other circumstances would not allow it. affected him exceedingly—grateful sensibility he expressed the warmth of his attachm to them & that, and his inclination to them on every other future occasion.—

* Scenes which presented themselves in this nights march are not to be described — the dead — the dying — the groans — lamentation — and cry along the Road for those under the latter de: scriptions, endeavoured from the first commencement of the action — or rather confusion were enough to pierce a heart of adamant. — The gloom & horror of which was not a little encrea: sed by the impervious darkness occasioned by the close shade of thick woods which in places rendered it impossible for the two guides which attended to know when they were out of the track but by groping on the ground with their hands.

⊛ being expected at the rivers part the Capt.n of the Party had gone across to his obsy in the mean time in the opposite direction I passed & escaped alm: certain destruction for the weather was raining and the few Carbines unfit for use — this happened near Fort Vass.

Page 8

(1). I believe about 7000 Bush.ds of Wheat and 10000 bushels of Ind.n Corn which was more the staple of the farm

Page 11

(2) Whether it be necessary to mention that my limited Services were given to the public without compensation and that every direct and indirect attempt afterwards, to reward them as appeared by the Letter of J. Mifflin — and the vote of 50 shares in each of the navigations of Potomack & James River by the State of Virg.a who knew that I would refuse any thing that should carry with it the appearance of reward — you can best judge. —

Page 14

(1). once a week is his fixed hunts tho sometimes he goes oftener.

(2) and many others in this Country

(3) regarding the State of the Weather — nature of the Soil &c.

☞ The information given in these sheets — tho related from memory, I believe it to be depended upon. — It is hastily and incorrectly related — but not so much for those reasons, as some others of it, is my earnest request, that after Col. Humphreys has selected what he shall judge necessary, and given it in his own Language, that the whole of what is here contained may be returned to me, or committed to the flames. — some of the enumerations are trifling, and perhaps more important circumstances omitted; — but just as they occurred to the memory, they were committed. If there are any grains among them Col. H. can easily seperate them from the chaff.

Washington Papers

given to me by Wm Hum-
phreys — 1849 —

containing original
memos in Washington's
handwriting; by way
of remarks upon some
intended biography of
which Genl Humphreys
was writing
Jno Pickering

George Washington's

"REMARKS"

It was rather the wish of my eldest brother (on whom the general concerns of the family devolved) that this shd take place & the mat<ter> was contemplated by him—My father died when I was only 10 years old.[1]

He was not appointed Adjutant General of the Militia of Virginia untill after his return from the expedition to Carthagena—Nor did he Command the Colonial troops on that occasion—these were under the Orders of Sir Wm. Gouch Lt Govr of Virginia—He was no more than the Senior Officer of those which were raised in this Colony & wch with those of the other Colonies formed what was called the American Brigade—under Sir William Gouch—he was scarcely of age when he went on this expedn.[2]

and from whom he had received many distinguished marks of patronage & favor.[3]

Not all—for the second Son (Augustine) left many childn, sevl of whom are now living; and inherit a very large portion of his Fathers Estate. perhaps the best part.[4]

Before he was 20 years of age.[5]

He was then more than 21 years—as will appear from dates.[6]

at a most inclement Season, for he travelled over the Apalacheon Mountains, and passed 250 miles thro an uninhabited wilderness Country (except by a few tribes of Indians settled on the Banks of the Ohio) to Presque Isle within 15 Miles of Lake Erie in the depth of winter when the face of the Earth was covered with snow and the waters covered with Ice; The whole dist[anc]e from Wmsburgh the then seat of Governmt at least 500 miles.[7]

It was on this occasion he was named by the half-King (as he was called) and the tribes of Nations with whom he treated—Caunotaucarius (in English) the Town taker; which name being registered in their Manner & communicated to other Nations of Indians, has been remembered by them ever since in all their transactions with him during the late war.[8]

This is a task to which G.W. feels himself very incompetent (with any degree of accuracy) from the badness of his memory—loss of Papers—mutilated state, in which those of that date were preserved—and the derangement of them by frequent removals in the late war & want of time to collect and methodize them since.[9] However accordg to the best of his recollection: By the indefatigable Industry of the Lt Colo. and the Officers who seconded his measures the Regiment[10] was in great forwardness at Alexandria (the place of general rendezvous) early in the spring of 1754 and without waiting till the whole should be completed—or for a detachment from the Independent Companies of regulars[11] in the Southern Provences (which had been <reqd> by the Executive of Virginia[12] for this Service) or for troops which were raising in North Carolina[13] and destined in conjunction to oppose the Incroachment of the French on our Western frontiers—He began his March in the Month of May in order to open the Roads, and this he had to do almost the whole distance *from Winchester*[14] (in the County of Frederick not more than 80 miles from Alexandria to the Ohio)—For deposits—&ca—and for the especiall purpose of siezing, if possible, before the French shd arrive at it, the important Post at the conflux[15] of the Alligany and Monongahela; with the advantages of which he was forcibly struck the preceeding year; and earnestly advised the securing of with Militia,[16] or some other temporary force. But notwithstanding all his exertions, the New, and uncommon difficulties he had to encounter (made more intolerable by incessant Rains and swelled waters of which he had many to cross) he had but just ascended the Lawrel Hill[17] 50 M: short of his object: after a March of 230 Miles from Alexa. when he received information from his Scouts that the French had in force, siezed the Post[18] he was pushing to obtain; having descended from Presque Isle by the Rivers Le beouf[19] and Alligany to this Place by water with artillery &ca &ca—The object of his precipitate advance being thus defeated—The detachmt of regulars, wch had arrived at Alexa. (by water) and under his orders being far in his rear—and no Acct of the

Troops from No. Carolina—it was thought advisable to fall back a few miles, to a place known by the name of the great meadows[20]—abounding in Forage more convenient for the purpose of forming a Magazine & bringing up the rear—and to advance from (if we should ever be in force to do it) to the attack of the Post which the enemy now occupied; and had called Du Quesne[21]—At this place, some days after, we were joined by the above detachment of regulars; consisting (before they were reduced on the March by desertion, Sickness &ca) of a Captn (McKay a brave & worthy Officer)[22]—three Subalterns—and 100 Rank & file. But previous to this junction the French sent a detachment to reconnoitre our Camp to obtain intelligence of our strength & position; notice of which being given by the Scouts G.W. marched at the head of a party, attacked, killed 9 or 10; & captured 20 odd.[23] This, as soon as the enemy had assembled their Indian allies, brought their whole force upon him; consisting, according to their own compared with the <best> accts that could be obtained from others of about 1500 Men[24]—His force consisted of the detachment above mentioned, and between two & 300 Virginians; for the few Indians which till now had attended <him,> and who by reconnoitering the enemy on their March had got terrified at their numbers and resolved to retreat as they advised us to do also but which was impracticable without abandoning our Stores—Baggage—&ca as the horses which had brought them to this place had returned for Provision had left us previous to the Attack.[25] About 9 Oclock on the 3d of July the Enemy advanced with Shouts, & dismal Indian yells to our Intrenchments, but was opposed by so warm, spirited, & constant a fire, that to force the works in that way was abandoned by them—they then, from every little rising—tree—Stump—Stone—and bush kept up a constant galding fire upon us; which was returned in the best manner we could till late in the afternn when their fell the most tremendous rain that can be conceived—filled our trenches with water—wet, not only the ammunition in Cartouch boxes and firelocks, but that which was in a small temporary Stockade in the middle of the Intrenchment called Fort necessity[26] erected for the sole purpose of its security, and that of the few stores we had; and left us nothing but a few (for all were not provided with them) Bayonets for defence.[27] In this situation & no prosp[ec]t of bettering it[,] terms of capitulation[28] were offered to us by the ene<my> wch with some alterations that were insisted upon were the more readily acceded to, as we had no Salt provisions, & but indifferently supplied with fresh; which, from

George Washington's
"REMARKS"

17

the heat of the weather, would not keep; and because a full third of our numbers Officers as well as privates were, by this time, killed or wounded—The next Morning we marched out with the honors of War[29], but were soon plundered contrary to the articles of capitulation of great part of our Baggage by the Savages. Our Sick and wounded were left with a detachment under the care, and command of the worthy Doctr Craik (for he was not only Surgeon to the Regiment but a lieutt therein[)][30] with such necessaries as we could collect and the Remains of the Regimt, and the detachment of Regulars, took up their line for the interior Country. And at Winchester met 2 Companies from No. Carolina on their March to join them—These being fresh, & properly provided, were ordered to proceed to Wills's Creek & establish a post (<since> called Fort Cumberland)[31] for the purpose of covering the Frontiers, Where they were joined by a Company from Maryland[32], which, about this time, had been raized—Captn McKay with his detachment remd at Winchester; & the Virginia Regiment proceedd to Alexandria in order to recruit, & get supplied with cloathing & necessarys of which they stood much in need. In this manner the Winter was employed, when advice was recd of the force destined for this Service under the ordrs of G.B.[33] and the arrival of Sir Jno. St Clair the Q: Mastr Genl[34] with some new arrangement of Rank by which no officer who did not *immediately* derive his Comn from the King could command one who did—This was too degrading for G.W. to submit to; accordingly, he resigned his Military employment;[35] determining to serve the next campaign as a Volunteer; but upon the arrival of Genl Braddock he was very particularly noticed by that General—taken into his family as an extra-Aid[36]—offered a Captns Comn by *brevet* (which was the highest Grade he had it in his power to bestow[)] and had the compliment of several blank Ensigncies given him to dispose of to the Young Gentlemen of his acqe to supply the vacancies in the 44 and 48 Regts which had arrived from Ireland.[37]

In this capacity he commenced his second Campaign and used every proper occasion till he was taken Sick[38] & left behind in the vicinity of Fort Cumberland to impress the Genl, & the principal Officers around him, with the necessity of opposing the nature of his defence, to the mode of attack which, more than probably, he would experience from the *Canadian* French,[39] and their Indians on his March through the Mountains & covered Country but so prepossed were they in favr of *regularity & disci-*

pline and in such absolute contemp<t> were *these people held,* that the admonition was suggested in vain.

About the middle of June, this Armament consisting of the two Regiments from Ireland—some Independant Companies and the Provincial troops of Virga Maryld & North Carolina,[40] began to move from Fort Cumberland whither they had assembled—after several days March; and difficulties to which they had never been accustomed in regular Service, in Champaign Countries;[41] and of whh they seemed to have had very little idea—the Genl resolved to divide his force,[42] and at the head of the first division which was composed of the flower of his Army, to advance; and leave Colo. Dunbar[43] with the second division & the heavy Baggage & Stores, to follow after. By so doing, the first division approached the Monongahela 10 miles short of Fort Duquesne the 8th of July; at which time and place having so far recovered from a severe fever and delerium from which he had been rescued by James's powder,[44] administed by the positive order of the Genl as to travel in a covered Waggon, he joined him and the next day tho much reduced and very weak mounted his horse on cushions, & attended as one of his aids.

About 10 Oclock on the 9th, after the Van had crossed the Monongahela the second time,[45] to avoid an ugly defile[46] (the season being very dry & waters low) and the rear yet in the River the front was attacked; and by the unusual Hallooing[47] and whooping of the enemy, whom they could not see, were so disconcerted and confused, as soon to fall into irretrievable disorder. The rear was forced forward to support them, but seeing no enemy, and themselves falling every moment from the fire, a general panic took place among the Troops from which no exertions of the Officers could recover them[48]—In the early part of the Action some of the Irregulars (as they were called) *without direc<t>ns* advanced to the right, in loose order, to attack; but this, *unhappily* from the unusual appearance of the movement being mistaken for cowardice and a running away was discountenanced—and before it was *too late, &* the confusion became general an offer was made by G.W. to head the Provincials, & engage the enemy in their own way; but the propriety of it was not seen into until it was too late for execution[.] after this, many attempts were made to dislod<ge> the enemy from an eminence on the Right[49] but they all proved eneffectual; and fatal to the Officers who by great exertions and good examples endeavourd to accomplish it. In one of these the Genl recd the Wd of which he died;[50] but previous to it,

George Washington's
"REMARKS"

had several horses killed & disabled under him. Captns Orme[51] & Morris[52] his two Aids de Camp having received wounds which rendered them unable to attd G.W. remained the sole aid through the day, to the Genl; he also had one horse killed, and two wounded under him—A ball through his hat—and several through his clothes, but escaped unhurt. Sir Peter Halket (secd in Command) being early killed[53]—Lieutt Colo. Burton[54] & Sir Jno. St Clair (who had the Rank of Lt Colo. in the Army) being badly wounded—Lieutt Colo. Gage (afterwards Genl Gage) having recd a contusion[55]—No person knowing in the disordered State things were who the Surviving Senr Officer was & the Troops by degrees going off in confusion; without a ray of hope left of further opposition from those that remained; G.W. placed the Genl in a small covered Cart, which carried some of his most essential equipage, and in the best order he could, with the last Troops (who only contind to be fired at) brought him over the first ford of the Monongahela; where they were formed in the best order circumstances would admit on a piece of rising ground; after wch, by the Genls order, he rode forward to halt those which had been earlier in the retreat: Accordingly, after crossing the Monongahela the *second time* and ascending the heights, he found Lieutt Colo. Gage engaged in this business to whom he delivered the Genls order and then returned to report the situation he found them in—When he was again requested by the Genl whom he met coming on, in his litter with the first halted troops, to proceed (it then being after sundown) to the second division under the command of Colo. Dunbar, to make arrangements for covering the retreat, and forwarding on provisions & refreshments to the retreating & wounded Soldiery—To accomplish this, for the 2d division was 40 odd miles in the rear it took up the whole night & part of the next morning—which from the weak state in which he was, and the fatiegues, and anxiety of the last 24 hours, rendered him in a manner wholly unfit for the execution of the duty he was sent upon when he arrived at Dunbars Camp[56]—To the best of his power however, he discharged it, and remained with the secd division till the other joined it. The shocking Scenes which presented themselves in this Nights March are not to be described— The dead—the dying—the groans—lamentation—and crys along the Road of the wounded for help (for those under the latter descriptions endeavoured from the first commencement of the action—or rather confusion to escape to the 2d divn) were enough to pierce a heart of adamant. the gloom & horror of which was not a little encreased by the impervious darkness occasioned by the close shade of thick woods which in places rendered it impossible for the two guides which attended to know when they were in, or out of the track but by groping on the ground with their hands.

Happy was it for him, and the remains of the first division that they left such a quantity of valuable and enticing baggage on the field as to occasion a scramble and contention in the seizure & distribution of it among the enemy for had a pursuit taken place—by passing the defile which we had avoided; and they had got into our rear, the whole, except a few woodsmen, would have fallen victims to the merciless Savages—Of about 12 or 13 hundred which were in this action eight or 9 hundd were either killed or wounded; among whom a large proportion of brave & valuable Officers were included—The folly & consequence of opposing compact bodies to the sparse manner of Indian fighting, in woods, which had in a manner been predicted, was now so clearly verified that from hence forward another mode obtained in all future operations.

As soon as the two divisions united, the whole retreated towards Fort Cumberland; and at an Incampment near the Great Meadows the brave, but unfortunate Genl Braddock breathed his last. He was interred with the honors of war, and as it was left to G.W. to see this performed, & to mark out the spot for the reception of his remains—to guard against a savage triumph, if the place should be discovered—they were deposited in the Road over which the Army, Waggons &ca passed to hide every trace by which the entombment could be discovered.[57] Thus died a man, whose good & bad qualities were intimately blended. He was brave even to a fault and in regular Service would have done honor to his profession—His attachments were warm—his enmities were strong—and having no disguise about him, both appeared in full force. He was generous & disinterested—but plain and blunt in his manner even to rudeness—After this event, the Troops continued their March for, & soon arrived at Fort Cumberland without molestation: and all except the P[rovinci]als immediately resolved to proceed to Philadelphia;[58] by which means the Frontiers of that State but *more especially* those of Virginia and Maryland were laid *entirely* open by the *very avenue* which had been prepared.—Of the direful consequences of this measure G.W., in a visit wch he immediately made to Williamsburgh for the purpose brought the Govr & Council of Virga acquainted—But In vain did they remonstrate against the March of the B. Troops to that place to the Officer com[mandin]g them.

George Washington's
"REMARKS"

They proceeded to augment their own: the command of which under a very & enlarged & dignified Commission, to Command *all* the Troops now raised, or to be raised in the Colony, was given to him with very extensive powers, and blank Commissions to appoint all New Officers.[59] About this time also or soon after it the discontents and clamours of the Provincial Officers, and the remonstrance of G.W. in person, to Genl Shirley, the then Comr in chief of the British Forces in America[60] and through the Govr & Council to the Kings Minister[61] with respect to the degrading Situation in which they were placed[,] a new arrangement took place by the Kings order, by which every Provincial Officer was to rank according to the Comn he bore, but to be junr to those of the same grade in the established Corps.

As G.W. foresaw, so it happened, the frontiers were continually harrassed—but not having force enough to carry the war to the gates of Du Quesne, he could do no more than distribute the Troops along the Frontiers in Stockaded Forts; more with a view to quiet the fears of the Inhabitants than from any expectation of giving security on so extensive a line to the settlements. During this interval in one of his tours along the frontier posts—he narrowly escaped, according to the acc. afterwards given by some of our People who were Prisoners with them, and eyewitness at the time <of the parties falling> by an Indian party who had waylaid (for another purpose) the communication along which with a small party of horse only he was passing—the road in this place formed a curve—and the prey they were in weight for being expected at the reverse part, the Captn of the party had gone across to observe the number [and] manner of their movemt &ca in order that he might make his disposition accordingly leaving orders for the party not to take notice of any passengers the other <way> till he returned to them—in the mean time in the opposite direction I passed & escaped almt certain destruction for the weather was raining and the few Carbines unfit for use if we had escaped the first fire—This happened near Fort Vass.[62] Never ceasing in the mean time in his attempts, to demonstrate to the Legislature of Virga—to Lord Loudoun[63]—&ca that the only means of preventing the devastations to which the middle states were exposed, was to remove the cause. But the war by this time raging in another quarter of the Continent all applications were unheeded till the year 1758 when an Expedition against Fort Du Quesne was concerted, and undertaken under the conduct of Genl Forbes;[64] who tho a brave & good Officer, was so much debilitated by bad health, and so illy supplied with the means to carry on the expedition, that it was November before the Troops got to Loyalhanning:[65] 50 or 60 miles short of Duquesne & even then was on the very point of abandoning the Exhibition when some seasonable supplies arriving the Army was formed into three Brigades took up its March—and moved forward; the Brigade Commanded by G.W. being the leading one.[66]

Previus to this, and during the time the Army lay at Loyalhaning a circumstance occurred wch involved the life of G.W. in as much jeopardy as it had ever been before or since[.][67] the enemy sent out a large detachment to reconnoitre our Camp, and to ascertain our strength; in consequence of Intelligence that they were within 2 Miles of the Camp a party commanded by Lt Colo. Mercer[68] of the Virga line (a gallant & good Officer) was sent to dislodge them between whom a Severe conflict & hot firing ensued which lasting some time & appearing to approach the Camp it was conceived that our party was yielding the ground upon which G.W. with permission of the Genl called (for dispatch) for Volunteers and immediately marched at their head to sustain, as was conjectured the retiring troops. led on by the firing till he came within less than half a mile, & it ceasing, he detached Scouts to investigate the cause & to communicate his approach to his friend Colo. Mercer advancing slowly in the meantime—But it being near dusk and the intelligence not having been fully dissiminated among Colo. Mercers Corps, and they taking us, for the enemy who had retreated approaching in another direction commenced a heavy fire upon the releiving party which drew fire in return in spite of all the exertions of the Officers one of whom & several privates were killed and many wounded[69] before a stop could be put to it. to accomplish which G.W. never was in more imminent danger by being between two fires, knocking up with his sword the presented pieces.

When the Army had got within about 12 or 15 miles of the Fort the enemy dispairing of its defence, blew it up—having first embarked their Artillery Stores & Troops—and retreated by water down the Ohio to their Settlements below—thus ended that Campaign, a little before Christmas in very inclement weather; and the last one made during that War by G.W.[70] whose health by this time (as it had been declining for many months before occasioned by an inveterate disorder in his Bowels) became so precarious as to induce him (having seen quiet restored by this event to the Frontiers of his own Country which was the principal inducement to his taking arms) to resign his Military appointments— The sollicitation of the Troops which he commanded to Con-

George Washington's
" R E M A R K S "

tinue—their Affecte farewell address[71]—to him, when they found the Situation of his health and other circumstances would not allow it affected him exceedingly and in grateful sensibility he expressed the warmth of his attachmt to them on that, and his inclination to serve them on every other future occasion.[72]

I beleive about 7,000 Bushls of Wheat and 10,000 bushels of Indn Corn which was more the staple of the farm.[73]

Whether it be necessary to mention that my time & Services were given to the public without compensation, and that every direct and indirect attempt afterwards, to reward them (as appeared by the Letter of G. Mifflin—and the vote of 50 shares in each of the Navigations of Potomack & James River by the State of Virga who knew that I would refuse any thing that should carry with it the appearance of reward[)]—you can best judge.[74]

(1). once a week is his fixed hunts tho sometimes he goes oftner.[75]

(2) and many others in this Country[76]

(3) remarking the state of the Weather—nature of the Soil &ca[77]

The information given in these sheets—tho related from Memory, It is I believe to be depended upon. It is hastily and incorrectly related—but not so much for these reasons, as some others, it is earnest<ly> requestd that after Colo. Humphreys has extracted what he shall judge necessary, and given it in his own language, that the *whole* of what Is here contained may be returned to G.W., or committed to the flames.—some of the enumerations are trifling; and perhaps more important circumstances omitted; but just as they occurred to the memory, they were committed—If there are any grains among them Colo. H. can easily seperate them from the chaff.

George Washington

R E M E M B E R S

[Inscription on wrapper, by John Pickering (1777–1846)]

Washington — Paper –
given to me by Mrs [Ann Frances Bulkeley] Humphreys 1829 containing original memos. in Washington's handwriting by way of remarks upon an intended biography which Genl Humphreys was writing—
Jno. Pickering

Martin West

Director, Fort Ligonier

Annotation

1. Washington's comment refers to this passage by David Humphreys: "*As it was the design of his Father that he should be bred for an Officer in the British navy, his mental acquisitions & exterior accomplishments were calculated to give him distinction in that profession.*" Rosemarie Zagarri, ed., *David Humphreys' "Life of General Washington" with George Washington's "Remarks"* (Athens, Ga., 1991), 7.

The possibility that George Washington might enter the British navy at age fourteen occurred in the autumn of 1746, three years after the death of his father Augustine (1694–1743). As noted in his "Remarks," George's half brother Lawrence (*c.*1718–1752) was the one who encouraged him to go to sea as a midshipman. Although initially in favor of the plan, George's mother, Mary Ball Washington (*c.*1708–1789), greatly influenced by her half brother, Joseph Ball II (1689–1760), came to express her disapproval and the idea was abandoned. Frank E. Grizzard, Jr., *George Washington: A Biographical Companion* (Santa Barbara, Calif., 2002), "Washington, Lawrence," 331–332, 403, 409.

2. Washington's comment refers to this passage by David Humphreys: "*The Father of General Washington had three sons by a former wife. The eldest [Lawrence Washington], a young man of the most promising talents, after having been appointed Adjutant General of the Militia of Virginia, commanded the Colonial troops in the expedition against Carthagena.*" Zagarri, *Humphreys' "Life of General Washington"*: 8.

Augustine Washington, the father of George Washington, was born at Mattox Creek, Virginia. In 1715, he married Jane Butler (1699–1729) of Westmoreland County, Virginia; four children were born to the couple: Butler (b. and d. *c.*1716), Lawrence,

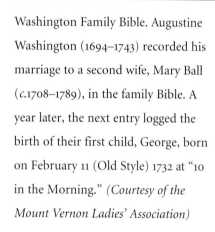

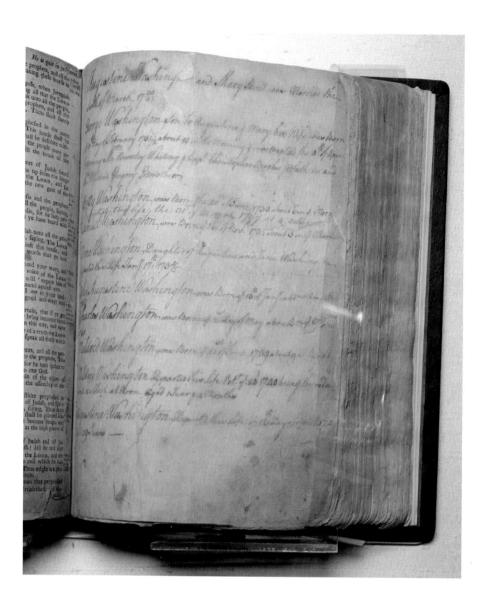

George Washington

REMEMBERS

Washington Family Bible. Augustine Washington (1694–1743) recorded his marriage to a second wife, Mary Ball (*c.*1708–1789), in the family Bible. A year later, the next entry logged the birth of their first child, George, born on February 11 (Old Style) 1732 at "10 in the Morning." *(Courtesy of the Mount Vernon Ladies' Association)*

Augustine (1720–1762), and Jane (*c.*1722–1735), but in 1729 their mother died. Augustine Washington remarried two years later, and his wife, Mary Ball Washington, gave birth to George Washington on February 11 (Old Style), 1732.

Lawrence Washington, the elder surviving half brother of George, fought in the Anglo-Spanish War of Jenkins's Ear (1739–1743). He was commissioned in 1740 a captain in one of four Virginia companies, which were raised to serve in the American Foot Regiment for overseas service led by Sir William Gooch (1681–1751), the lieutenant governor of Virginia from 1727 to 1749. Washington participated in the failed Anglo-American assault on Cartagena de Indias (today a city in Colombia), a flourishing Spanish port on the Caribbean Sea, in spring 1741. Returned home, he was appointed adjutant general of Virginia in 1743, which conferred the rank of major. The primary duty of this position was to provide a rudimentary training and education in the art of war to the militia companies of each county. Lawrence

Sir William Gooch, unattributed. Sir William Gooch (1681–1751) was lieutenant governor of Virginia for over two decades (1727–1749). During the War of Jenkins's Ear (1739–1743), he commanded the American Foot Regiment and a young captain of Virginia troops named Lawrence Washington. *(Colonial Williamsburg Foundation, Accession number 2000-39)*

Annotation

Washington died from pulmonary disease in 1752. Grizzard, *George Washington: A Biographical Companion,* "Washington, Augustine," 326–327, "Washington, Lawrence," 331–332; W. W. Abbot et al., eds., *The Papers of George Washington, Colonial Series, 1748–August 1755* (Charlottesville, Va., 1983), 1: 51 n.3; *American National Biography* (New York, 1999), 9, "Gooch, Sir William": 229–230.

3. Washington's comment refers to this passage by Humphreys: "*and on his return [from Cartagena, Lawrence Washington] called his patrimonial Mansion, Mount Vernon, in honour of the Admiral of that name with whom he had contracted a particular intimacy.*" Zagarri, *Humphreys' "Life of General Washington"*: 8.

In 1743, Lawrence Washington was heir to the family tract of land at Little Hunting Creek, where he renamed the residence Mount Vernon, after Admiral Edward Vernon (1684–1757), the British commander on the unsuccessful Cartagena operation. Alan Gallay, *Colonial Wars of North America, 1512–1763: An Ency-*

clopedia (New York, 1996), "Vernon, Edward," 758; Grizzard, *George Washington: A Biographical Companion*, "Washington, Lawrence," 331–332.

4. Washington's comment refers to this passage by Humphreys: "*On the death of all the children by the first marriage, General Washington acceded to a large landed property.*" Zagarri, *Humphreys' "Life of General Washington,"* 8.

Augustine Washington was the younger of George's two elder half brothers. As Washington mentioned in his "Remarks," Augustine and Anne Aylett Washington (d. *c.*1773) were survived by several children: William Augustine (1747–1810), Elizabeth (1750–1814), Ann (1752–1777), Jane (1756–1833) and George (b. *c.*1758). Grizzard, *George Washington: A Biographical Companion*, "Washington, Augustine," 328, 408.

5. Washington's comment refers to this passage by Humphreys: "*in consequence of the vacancy in the Office of Adjutant General & of the extensive limits of the Colony, the Office was divided into three districts, and the future hero of America began his military career by a principal appointment in that Department, with the rank of Major.*" Zagarri, *Humphreys' "Life of General Washington,"* 8.

On June 16, 1752, prior to Lawrence Washington's death, George Washington importuned the Lieutenant Governor of Virginia, Robert Dinwiddie (1693–1770), to consider him as a candidate for the position of adjutant general of the one of four newly created militia districts, the Northern Neck (the peninsula between the Potomac and Rappahannock rivers) and Eastern Shore. Through the reputation and lingering influence of his late elder half brother and the interest of the powerful Fairfax family into which Lawrence had married, on November 6, 1752, Washington was appointed adjutant of the Southern District with the rank of major. Washington was eventually transferred to his desired adjutancy of the Northern Neck and Eastern Shore District. *PGW, Col. Ser.*, 1: 39, 50–51n.3, 55, 77n.5.

6. Washington's comment refers to this passage by Humphreys: "*When he was little more than twenty one years of age, an event [Washington's diplomatic mission to the French forts in northwestern Pennsylvania] occurred, which called his abilities into public notice.*" Zagarri, *Humphreys' "Life of General Washington,"* 9.

Washington, as the adjutant general of the Southern District of Virginia with the rank of major, was authorized by Lieutenant Governor Dinwiddie in October 1753 to carry a summons to the French troops occupying two new forts, Machault (modern

Franklin, Pennsylvania), named for Jean-Baptiste Machault d'Arnouville (1701–1794), minister of the marine, 1754–1757, and de la Rivière au Boeuf (present Waterford, Pennsylvania) on French Creek, a tributary of the Allegheny River. To assert royal authority on lands claimed by Virginia, the demand was for an immediate evacuation. The British feared that the French intended both to dominate the rich fur trade and to secure the physical connection, and thus the interests, of Canada and Louisiana via the Ohio River, *La Belle Rivière.* The "junction" of these two vast French provinces was viewed with great alarm by both the British and Americans. In the event of a rejection, London authorized "Force of Arms" to implement this aggressive new policy. *PGW, Col. Ser.,* 1: 56–58.

7. Washington's comment refers to this passage by Humphreys: "*Young Mr Washington, who, was sent with plenary powers to ascertain the facts, to treat with the Savages, and to warn the French to desist from their aggressions, performed the duties of his Mission with singular industry, intelligence & address.*" Zagarri, *Humphreys' "Life of General Washington,"* 9.

Bodleian Plate, *c.* 1740. The Virginia capital at Williamsburg boasted an impressive Governor's Palace often visited by George Washington when he went to see Lieutenant Governor Robert Dinwiddie. The only contemporary image of the building (*far right, second row*) is a copperplate engraving discovered in the Bodleian Library at Oxford University. (*Colonial Williamsburg Foundation, Accession number 1938–196*)

The rigorous journey led Major Washington from the capital at Williamsburg to Fort de la Rivière au Boeuf, which was a short distance south of Fort de la Presqu'île, "Fort of the Peninsula" (modern Erie, Pennsylvania). On October 31, Washington and a small party followed the common traders' path to the Forks of the Ohio, to arrive at nearby Logstown (present Baden, Pennsylvania). There, the major, joined by Tanaghrisson, the "Half-King" (d. 1754), was interrogated by the anxious Ohio peoples—Mingoes, Delawares, and Shawnees—as to the purpose of the visit; was he the vanguard of Anglo-American invaders who would steal their lands, or was he the representative of allies, who would preserve them from the French? Leaving the Forks, the group arrived at Fort Machault on December 4, 1753, and Captain Philippe Thomas Chabert de Joncaire (1707–c.1766) refused the summons, directing Washington north to Fort de la Rivière au Boeuf. Seven days later, the Virginian presented Dinwiddie's message to the commandant, Captain Jacques Legardeur de Saint Pierre (1701–1755), which asked in part, "by whose Authority and Instructions you have lately marched from Canada, with an armed Force, and invaded the King of Great-Britain's Territories, . . . It becomes my Duty to require your peaceable Departure." Diplomatically, the captain responded, "As to the Summons you send me to retire, I do not think myself obliged to obey it." Unsuccessful in his mission, Washington returned to Virginia. Donald H. Kent, *The French Invasion of Western Pennsylvania, 1753* (Harrisburg, 1954), 6, 10, 70–76; *PGW, Col. Ser.*, 1: 7, 56–57, 140n.21; Michael N. McConnell, *A Country Between: The Upper Valley and Its Peoples, 1724–1774* (Lincoln, Neb., 1992), 107–108; Joseph L. Peyser, *Jacques Legardeur de Saint-Pierre: Officer, Gentleman, Entrepreneur* (East Lansing, Mich., 1996), 4, 224; *The Journal of George Washington* (Williamsburg, Va., 1959), 25–27.

8. Washington's comment refers to this passage by Humphreys: "*But it was deemed by some an extraordinary circumstance that so young and inexperienced a Person should have been employed on a negotiation, with which subjects of the greatest importance were involved; subjects which shortly after became the origin of a war between the two Kingdoms of England & France, that raged for many years throughout every part of the world.*" Zagarri, *Humphreys' "Life of General Washington,"* 9–10.

Tanaghrisson, or Tanacharison (d. 1754), the "Half-King" of the Mingoes, was of mixed Seneca and Catawba (a southern, Siouan people) heritage. Tanaghrisson settled in the Ohio Country, the region which he later called "a Country between," the Iro-

quoian (or Six Nations) immigrants there being termed the Mingoes. Having risen to prominence as a diplomatic broker between
the Ohio peoples and the colonies of Pennsylvania and Virginia,
Tanaghrisson became known as the Half-King, a misleading English term for deputy of the Six Nations in the Upper Allegheny
region. His limited jurisdiction involved diplomacy and formal
gift-receiving, since the New York Iroquois retained little authority in the Ohio Country. Lacking real power as regent for the Six
Nations, the Half-King's actual control was confined to his own
village, Logstown, and kinship-based alliances with the other
Mingo settlements.

As the French established themselves on *La Belle Rivière* during 1753, Tanaghrisson, firmly aligned with the British, attempted
a resistance. When Fort de la Presqu'île was under construction
that summer, the Half-King encouraged the French to withdraw,
but in vain. In November and December he tried to build Mingo
support for British interests and accompanied Washington on his
diplomatic assignment to the French posts in northwestern Pennsylvania, but again without effect. He fought at what later became
known as Jumonville Glen May 28. Displaced from Logstown by
the French, Tanaghrisson found refuge at Aughwick Creek (modern Shirleysburg, Pennsylvania), where he died of pneumonia in
October 1754. McConnell, *A Country Between,* 110–111; Fred
Anderson, *Crucible of War: The Seven Years' War and the Fate of
Empire in British North America, 1754–1766* (New York, 2000),
60–61; *ANB,* 21, "Tanacharison," 292–293.

George Washington is believed to have been heir to the Seneca
title of Caunotaucarius, or Conotocarious, meaning "Destroyer of
Villages," "Town Devourer" or "Town Taker," a name which was
reportedly first given to his great-grandfather, John Washington (1632–1677) by the Susquehannocks, an Iroquoian people.
According to George Washington, Tanaghrisson gave him the
appellation Conotocarious sometime during November and December 1753. Although apparently receiving his Seneca name by
descent, Washington also earned the grim cognomen, Destroyer
of Villages, during the War for Independence. In 1779, to stem
severe British-Iroquoian attacks on American settlers in New York
and Pennsylvania, he ordered General John Sullivan (1740–1795)
to undertake a scorched earth policy against the people and lands
(today west-central New York State) of the Six Nations, as well as
authorizing an independent secondary strike on Seneca villages in
northwestern Pennsylvania. These offensives failed to curtail the
raids, but were a blow from which Iroquoia never fully recovered.

In 1790 the Seneca headman Gyantwahia, or Cornplanter (*c.*1740–1836), informed Conotocarious that "When your army entered the country of the Six Nations, we called you Town Destroyer and to this day when that name is heard our women look behind them and turn pale, and our children cling close to the necks of their mothers." Francis Jennings, "Glory, Death, and Transfiguration: The Susquehannock Indians in the Seventeenth Century," *Proceedings of the American Philosophical Society* 112, no. 1 (February 1968): 16, 34–35; *PGW, Col. Ser.*, 1: 88, 91n.8; *The Diaries of George Washington, 1748–65*, eds. Donald Jackson and Dorothy Twohig (Charlottesville, Va., 1976), I: 183–184n.37; Joseph R. Fischer, *A Well-Executed Failure: The Sullivan Campaign against the Iroquois, July–September 1779* (Columbia, S.C., 1997), 7; J. Frederick Fauz, "'Engaged in Enterprises Pregnant with Terror': George Washington's Formative Years Among the Indians" in Warren R. Hofstra, ed., *George Washington and the Virginia Backcountry* (Madison, Wis., 1998), 117–120, 127–128.

9. Washington's "task" was, in the words of his former aide-de-camp and intended biographer, David Humphreys (1752–1818) of Connecticut, to present briefly "the most interesting facts to this [diplomatic mission to the French] & the subsequent campaigns. . ." in 1754 and 1755 and "to annex similiar accounts after Braddock's defeat untill. . . [Washington's] leaving the service; if there should be any thing particularly worthy of preservation; according to the minute scale, on which this specimen of biography is intended." When the "Remarks" are compared with contemporary documents from 1753 through 1758, the general's memory of that period is generally accurate, if occasionally selective and incomplete. From Washington's perspective of the period in which he wrote his "Remarks," *circa* 1786–1788, "the late war" was the American Revolution, 1775–1783. Zagarri, *Humphreys' "Life of General Washington,"* 10.

10. In his "Remarks" Lieutenant Colonel Washington did not mention his immediate superior and the first commander of the Virginia Regiment, Colonel Joshua Fry (*c.*1700–1754). A native of England, Fry was professor of mathematics and natural philosophy at the College of William and Mary. On March 1, 1754, he was Dinwiddie's choice as colonel and "commander in Chief of the Virg[ini]a Regiment," a unit of six companies. During his subsequent three months of service, the colonel performed efficiently as an administrator, but in late May, when leading part of his regiment from Winchester to Wills Creek, Fry fell or was thrown from his horse, succumbing on the thirty-first to his injuries. Five

days later, Dinwiddie authorized the succession of Washington to the colonelcy and command of the Virginia Regiment. After the capitulation at the Great Meadows in July 1754, that October the Virginia Regiment was reorganized into ten independent companies to be led by captains; no field officers were authorized and an offended Washington promptly resigned. Following Braddock's defeat, Dinwiddie, in August 1755, recommissioned Washington colonel of the newly formed Virginia Regiment which was not disbanded until 1762. *PGW, Col. Ser.,* 1: 74n.3–75n.3, 126–127n.1; R. A. Brock, ed., *The Official Records of Robert Dinwiddie, Lieutenant Governor of the Colony of Virginia, 1751–1758* (Richmond, 1883–1884), II: 184–186; John R. Elting, ed., *Military Uniforms in America: The Era of the American Revolution, 1755–1795* (San Rafael, Calif., 1974), 20.

11. A number of Independent Companies—units assigned neither to a regiment nor to its administrative structure—was raised and thinly distributed across the British Isles and in the "Plantations" of Jamaica and Bermuda, as well as in South Carolina and New York. Many in the ranks had been drawn from elderly and infirm invalids. In 1754, four companies were stationed in New York and three companies in South Carolina, of which the Third and Fourth New York Companies and the Third South Carolina Company were sent to Pennsylvania. Stanley McCrory Pargellis, "The Four Independent Companies of New York," in Pargellis, ed., *Essays in Colonial History Presented to Charles McLean Andrews by his Students* (New Haven, Conn., 1931), 96–123.

12. The "Virginia Executive" at this time was Robert Dinwiddie, the lieutenant governor of the province, 1751–1758. Born near Glasgow, Scotland in 1692, Dinwiddie's work as a customs official in Bermuda led to his appointment as lieutenant governor in 1751. A stockholder in and strong advocate of the land speculation firm, the Ohio Company of Virginia, Dinwiddie initiated an aggressive stance against France in order to secure the Virginia frontiers and gain access to the fur trade of the transmontane region. Dinwiddie's orders to Washington in late 1753 to carry a summons to the French in northwestern Pennsylvania set in motion a sequence of events which ultimately ignited the Seven Years' War, and the young man emerged the following year an internationally known figure. His renown was increased when the lieutenant governor arranged the local publication of Washington's journal of the mission to Fort de la Rivière au Boeuf, a slim volume widely reprinted in colonial newspapers and appearing in a London edition in 1754. Shortly thereafter, Dinwiddie promoted Washington to lieu-

Annotation

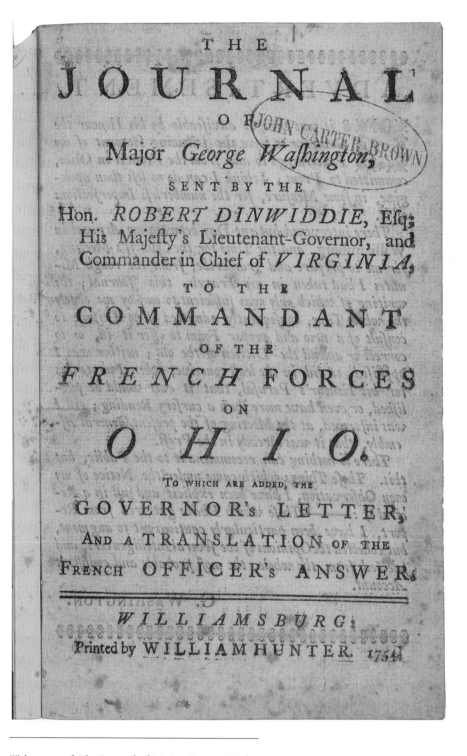

THE
JOURNAL
OF
Major *George Washington,*

SENT BY THE

Hon. *ROBERT DINWIDDIE,* Esq;
His Majesty's Lieutenant-Governor, and
Commander in Chief of *VIRGINIA,*

TO THE

COMMANDANT

OF THE

FRENCH FORCES

ON

OHIO.

To WHICH ARE ADDED, THE
GOVERNOR's LETTER,
AND A TRANSLATION OF THE
FRENCH OFFICER's ANSWER.

WILLIAMSBURG:
Printed by WILLIAM HUNTER. 1754.

Title page of *The Journal of Major George Washington,* 1754. Major Washington returned from his dangerous winter mission to Ohio Country with a journal and notes. Virginia Lieutenant Governor Dinwiddie, concerned by the French threat, hastily published the journal and made Washington an international celebrity at age twenty-two. *(Courtesy of the John Carter Brown Library at Brown University)*

tenant colonel and subsequently colonel of the Virginia Regiment, but the two men, the younger one sensitive and impulsive, the older one inflexible and magisterial, frequently clashed on matters of rank seniority, military-civil relations and finances. Dinwiddie remained an unwavering supporter of the war with France, but poor health led to his resignation and a return to England in 1758. *ANB*, 6; "Dinwiddie, Robert," 620–621.

13. To support Washington's operations in 1754, the government of North Carolina intended to raise a battalion of foot soldiers, totaling 750 men. This unit, however, never surpassed four hundred troops and arrived too late to participate in the action at the Great Meadows in July. *PGW, Col. Ser.*, 1: 92n.2, 195n.1–196n.2.

14. Winchester, Frederick County, Virginia became the site of a new fort in spring 1756 to serve as Washington's headquarters, which was named "Loudoun" to honor the incoming commander in chief in North America. Readily accessible to the Forks of the Ohio, Fort Loudoun facilitated the gathering of intelligence, Washington's highest priority; it also provided a civilian refuge and a central location for the establishment of a large magazine. *PGW, Col. Ser.*, 2: 352n.3; 3: 58–62, 278–280.

15. The "conflux," or confluence, of the Allegheny and Monongahela Rivers, then known as the Forks of the Ohio, forms the headwaters of the Ohio River at the center of modern Pittsburgh.

16. The militia was raised directly from the male citizenry of age, primarily for local or defensive purposes, organized into county units and theoretically prepared to protect the province. In January 1754, Lieutenant Governor Dinwiddie authorized Captain William Trent (1715–1787), an Ohio Company agent and veteran provincial officer, to recruit one hundred militiamen, primarily from Augusta County. In February, while at Redstone on the Monongahela River building a fortified storehouse for the land speculation firm, the Ohio Company of Virginia, Trent received orders from Dinwiddie to proceed forthwith to the Forks of the Ohio and build a small fort. *PGW, Col. Ser.*, 1: 63, 66n.2, n.4, 68, 93n.4.

17. Laurel Hill is a ridge of the Allegheny Mountains in southwestern Pennsylvania, and it extends fifty-five miles/ninety kilometers from the southwest to the northeast. Elevations average from 2,400 to 2,900 feet/732 to 855 meters, and two rivers, the Youghiogheny in the south and the Conemaugh in the north, cut through Laurel Hill. Archie Hobson, ed., *The Cambridge Gazetteer of the United States and Canada: A Dictionary of Places* (Cambridge, Mass., 2002), "Laurel Hill," 347.

Annotation

18. Captain Trent, having received new orders from Dinwiddie to move downriver to the headwaters of the Ohio, arrived there on February 17, 1754 and began construction of a stockade. Work was underway when he discovered in early April that the French were descending the Allegheny River in overwhelming force, with one thousand troops and native allies supported by eighteen pieces of artillery. They appeared at the Forks of the Ohio on April 16 and the following day the Virginians surrendered the unfinished Trent's Fort, also known as Fort Prince George after the Prince of Wales and future King George III (1738–1820). Charles Morse Stotz, *Outposts of the War for Empire: The French and English in Western Pennsylvania: Their Armies, Their Forts, Their People, 1749–1764* (Pittsburgh, 1985), 91; *PGW, Col. Ser.,* 1: 61–68, 83–85.

19. The *Rivière aux Boeufs,* "Beef (or Buffalo) River," was a tributary of the Allegheny River and was called French Creek by the British. Fort de la Rivière au Boeuf was built by the French in July 1753 at the south end of the portage road between Presqu'île and French Creek, positioned at the head of navigation for access south to the Ohio River. Stotz, *Outposts of the War for Empire,* 73–75.

20. The Great Meadows, located eleven miles east of modern Uniontown, Pennsylvania and immediately south of present US Route 40, was an open grassland in the broad valley situated between Chestnut Ridge to the west and Laurel Hill to the east. *PGW, Col. Ser.,* 1: 106n.1.

21. From its construction beginning in April 1753 to its demolition and abandonment in November 1758, Fort Duquesne was the largest of the four French posts in western Pennsylvania and headquarters for the security of *La Belle Rivière.* It was named for Ange de Menneville, Marquis de Duquesne (1702–1778), governor general of New France from 1752 to 1755. Stotz, *Outposts of the War for Empire,* 81–87.

22. James MacKay (d. 1785), believed to be a native of South Carolina, was commissioned ensign in the Independent Company of Foot of that province in 1737 and served in the War of Jenkins's Ear. On or about June 14, 1754, Captain McKay arrived with his command, the Third Independent Company of South Carolina, in western Pennsylvania to reinforce the Virginia Regiment at Fort Necessity, and on the night of July 3 he and Washington jointly signed the instrument of surrender. McKay resigned from the military the following year and sold his commission, moving to Georgia where he became a wealthy landowner. *PGW, Col. Ser.:* 77n.6.

23. On May 25, 1754, Ensign Joseph Coulon de Villiers de Jumonville (1718–1754) left the Forks of the Ohio on a diplomatic assignment to contact Washington and demand the removal of his troops from the region. On May 27, Washington learned that a small band of Frenchmen was encamped nearby, and, determined to strike first, he and Tanaghrisson left a covering force at Great Meadows to lead a detachment of forty provincials and Mingoes on a rainy night march. The following morning they ambushed the unsuspecting French from above a rocky glen in a skirmish of fifteen minutes. Ten of the surprised party, including Jumonville, were slain, one wounded and twenty-one captured, while one escaped; the ensign was reportedly tomahawked by the Half-King. Washington's losses were one killed and two or three wounded. The facts remain in dispute, but the French survivor reported that Jumonville was delivering his diplomatic summons to Washington when, without provocation, he was murdered by a discharge of small arms; Dinwiddie would blame Tanaghrisson and his Mingoes for this incident. Gallay, *Colonial Wars of North America*, "Coulon de Villiers de Jumonville, Joseph," 147–148; *PGW, Col. Ser.*, 1: 110–117; Anderson, *Crucible of War*, 5–7.

24. The late Jumonville's elder brother, Captain Louis Coulon de Villiers (1710–1757), informed of the May 28 ambush, arrived at Fort Duquesne on June 26. Intent on retribution, he took command of a powerful force, already assembled, to eject the Virginians from the Ohio Country. Two days later Villiers led about five hundred French and two hundred warriors, primarily Ottawas and Wyandots from the Great Lakes, but also some Ohioans, up the Monongahela Valley in pursuit of Washington. Gallay, *Colonial Wars of North America*, "Coulon de Villiers, Louis," 145–146; Anderson, *Crucible of War*, 64–65.

25. The prospect of French retaliation following the Jumonville ambush presented Tanaghrisson with no alternative except to remain temporarily with the British. In early June he and approximately eighty Mingoes were encamped at the Great Meadows, but they soon departed. The Half-King later explained that he had foreseen Washington would be caught at "that little thing [Fort Necessity] upon the Meadow," and suffer a humiliating defeat. The colonel, Tanaghrisson continued, was "a good-natured man," but untried, who, while striving vainly to instill regular discipline on the Mingoes, rejected their advice. McConnell, *A Country Between*, 110–111; Anderson, *Crucible of War*, 60–61.

26. Fort Necessity (near present Farmington, Pennsylvania) was a simple, basic work, constructed in haste by Washington and

Annotation

George Washington's French silver-mounted small sword, 1753–1754. George Washington imported this French sword from an English merchant in time to carry it during the 1755 campaign with General Braddock's army. The original wire-wrapping on the grip has disappeared. *(Courtesy of the Mount Vernon Ladies' Association)*

his Virginia Regiment, May 30–July 3, 1754 at the Great Meadows. This rudimentary fortification consisted of a circular stockade, fifty-three to fifty-four feet in diameter. Two low, earthen parapets, with shallow inner and outer trenches, together forming a diamond, protected approximately half the stockade. Under military duress, Washington aptly named this work "Fort Necessity." J. C. Harrington, *New Light on Washington's Fort Necessity: A Report on the Archeological Explorations at Fort Necessity National Battlefield Site* (Richmond, Va., 1957), 6–7, 32–34, 44–51.

27. On July 3, Villiers, having viewed the glen where his brother died and the remains of several unburied countrymen, arrived with his force before Fort Necessity. The defenders sallied from the works to deploy in formal line of battle because Washington expected a conventional engagement, but his adversaries closed to sixty yards and opened fire from the forest. In a driving rain, the Virginian withdrew to his fortifications, as the concealed attackers commenced a heavy musketry, sporadically answered by the partially exposed garrison. By dusk, Washington had lost over one hundred men, while Villiers suffered only three dead and seventeen wounded. Although the French were short on powder and lead, and their native allies grown restive, the heavy casualties suffered by the British, their inferior numbers, low provisions and the flooded condition of their fort rendered surren-

Dr. James Craik, unattributed. Scottish immigrant Dr. Craik (*c.* 1730–1814) served as an army surgeon with George Washington throughout the French and Indian War and the Revolutionary War. He was a lifelong friend and neighbor of the general and ministered to Washington as he died in 1799. (*Courtesy of Alexandria–Washington Lodge No. 22, AF & AM of Alexandria, Virginia. Photo: Arthur W. Pierson*)

der inevitable. Gallay, *Colonial Wars of North America,* "Coulon de Villiers, Louis," 146; *PGW, Col. Ser.,* 1: 159–160.

28. Without a formal state of war having yet been declared between France and England, Coulon de Villers, at 8 p.m. July 3, 1754, offered Washington a capitulation, which was a conditional surrender based on terms derived by mutual agreement between a besieging force and a garrison. In the process of reading aloud the instrument of surrender, Washington's interpreter, Jacob Van Braam (1725–1784), a Dutchman, inadvertently mistranslated two key French words, causing the Virginian to confess unwittingly to the "murder" of Jumonville. When this tacit, but mistaken, admission of guilt of assassination was learned in London, it was received with shock and dismay as "the most infamous a British subject ever put his hand to." *ANB,* 22, "Washington, George," 759; *PGW, Col. Ser.,* 1: 80n.5, 157–173.

29. Washington's capitulation at the Great Meadows included certain privileges granted by Coulon de Villiers known as "honors of war," in which the garrison was allowed to march out of Fort Necessity at drum beat, under arms and carrying a single artillery piece, one of nine light swivel guns that had defended the works.

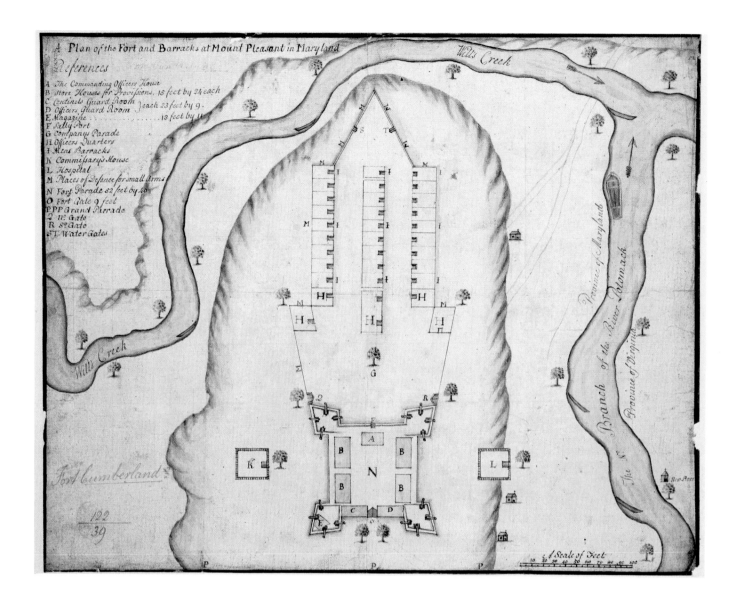

"Plan of Fort Cumberland," 1755. The sprawling Maryland provincial stockade became a royal fort, named for the Duke of Cumberland, when General Braddock's army stopped to prepare for its wilderness march in 1755. British military engineers were unimpressed with the fort but it remained an important depot and defense at the edge of the Allegheny Mountains until 1758. (By permission of the British Library, MAPS.K.Top 122.39)

Mark Mayo Boatner III, *Encyclopedia of the American Revolution* (New York, 1975), "Honors of War," 510.

30. James Craik (*c.*1730–1814), physician and military surgeon, was born in Kirkcudbright, Galloway, Scotland and studied medicine at the University of Edinburgh. He served with the Virginia Regiment as surgeon from 1754 to 1760, and developed a lifelong friendship with Washington. Craik also was Washington's personal doctor and cared for the former president at his deathbed in December 1799. *ANB*, 5, "Craik, James," 498–499.

31. Wills Creek (modern Cumberland, Maryland) referred to the vicinity surrounding the junction of the North Branch of the Potomac River and Wills Creek itself, which rises in west-central Pennsylvania and continues through western Maryland. The headquarters store for the Ohio Company had been erected there in late 1753, and a year later provincial forces built a stockade located on a ridge above Wills Creek. Commanded by a nearby mountain and isolated in the backcountry, this fort was expected partially to curtail the enemy raids on Maryland and Virginia,

and also to provide a military depot for the stockpile of supplies and stores. In 1755, General Edward Braddock renamed the post after the captain general of the British army, William Augustus, Duke of Cumberland (1721–1765). Fort Cumberland, expanded in size, served as Braddock's advance base. *PGW, Col. Ser.*, 1: 69n.1, 213n.3; Stotz, *Outposts of the War for Empire*, 91–94.

32. Immediately after the defeat at Fort Necessity, on July 16, 1754 the province of Maryland raised one hundred troops to support the Virginia forces. *PGW, Col. Ser.*, 1: 195n.1–196n.1.

33. Edward Braddock (1695–1755) was born in London and began his long army career in 1710, ultimately to attain the rank of major general in March 1754. Following a short tenure (twenty months) as governor of Gibraltar, in late 1754 he was made commander in chief of British forces in North America. Having served in the War of the Austrian Succession (1740–1748), but apparently having seen little action, Braddock's combat experience was limited; his superiors regarded him, however, as a capable administrator and a strict disciplinarian who was politically trustworthy. Braddock was ordered by the man who had selected him, the captain general, the Duke of Cumberland, to cut a road across the Allegheny Mountains, seize Fort Duquesne at the Forks of the Ohio, and then to move north against the enemy-held forts on French Creek. He met with an unexpected, disastrous defeat by a numerically inferior Franco-native force on the Monongahela River, six miles from the Forks, on July 9, 1755, and was mortally wounded in the total rout of his army. The event shocked the thirteen colonies, and damaged the inhabitants' faith in the British military. To many contemporary Americans and to succeeding generations of historians, writers, and antiquarians, Braddock, who lost not only the one battle in which he was ever to command, but also his own life, exemplified the ultimate in an inflexible, arrogant, and incompetent British officer, unwilling to conform to the realities of the American environment and enemy. Although much maligned, Braddock nevertheless successfully opened a new road in the backcountry and conducted his expedition with a certain military skill until the fatal encounter. *ANB*, 3, "Braddock, Edward," 349–350.

34. Sir John St. Clair (d. 1767), deputy quartermaster general in North America, was born in Fifeshire, Scotland. In 1726 he deemed himself heir to a title and was regarded so by many in Europe and North America, but no documentation of the creation of his Scottish baronetcy has been located. After service in the War of the Austrian Succession, St. Clair received the much-prized post of deputy quartermaster general in late 1754. On the

Annotation

George Washington

REMEMBERS

Sir John St. Clair, 1759, miniature by John Singleton Copley. John St. Clair (d. 1767) served with distinction as Deputy Quartermaster General for British forces in North America throughout both the 1755 Braddock Expedition (when he was seriously wounded) and the 1758 Forbes Campaign. Never overly fond of Americans, St. Clair had a reputation for both competence and irascibility. *(Courtesy of the Historical Society of Pennsylvania Collection, Atwater Kent Museum of Philadelphia)*

1755 expedition against Fort Duquesne, St. Clair, responsible for logistics, reconnaissance, provisioning, and roadbuilding, impressed Braddock with his performance. At the Monongahela on July 9, St. Clair, having almost completed the new road to the Forks of the Ohio that extended back to Fort Cumberland, was shot through the chest, "under the right pap," not long after the start of the engagement. Fully recovered, he served in the Forbes expedition in 1758, and St. Clair remained in America for the remainder of his life. Charles R. Hildenbrun, "Sir John St. Clair, Baronet, Quarter-Master General in America, 1753 to 1767," *The Pennsylvania Magazine of History and Biography* IX, no. 1 (1885): 1–14; *PGW, Col. Ser.*, 1: 295n.1.

35. Washington did not mention that due to a reorganization of the Virginia Regiment, he had actually resigned as colonel in late October of 1754, long before Braddock's arrival in North America. In coordination with instructions from London, Dinwiddie reduced Washington's command into unregimented com-

panies, which meant that no officer could be ranked above captain. Even if the officers of these new independent companies of Virginia were given regular king's commissions, which was expected but never realized, Washington had no intention of serving under the captains of the British Independent Companies of New York and South Carolina, whom he had led the previous year. *PGW, Col. Ser.*, 1: 224.

36. Braddock's two principal aides were English regular officers, but the general wanted Washington to participate in some capacity in his command. Washington rejected the general's offer of a brevet (honorary) captaincy as demeaning to one who had held a provincial colonelcy, but accepted the role of extra aide due to his esteem for Braddock. Acting as a volunteer at his own expense, an arrangement often used in the British military, Washington hoped to gain distinction in action and receive preferment from the general in the form of a regular field officer's commission in the king's service. Richard Bowyer, *Dictionary of Military Terms* (London, 1999), 6.

37. The Forty-fourth and Forty-eighth Regiments of Foot were maintained on the Irish Establishment, a largely autonomous military organization of twelve thousand British officers and men, funded by the Dublin Parliament and administered by the resident head of state, the lord lieutenant. The Test Act of 1673 legally barred Roman Catholics and Presbyterians from military service, and accordingly most of the British troops in Ireland were not ethnically Irish but recruited primarily in England, Scotland, and Wales. In late 1754, Cumberland ordered two regiments from Ireland, the Forty-fourth and the Forty-eighth, to be transported to America as the core of Braddock's army. The two units were in their depleted Irish status, separately consisting of ten companies, each of which contained a captain, a lieutenant, an ensign, two sergeants, two corporals, a drummer, and twenty-nine privates. In order to equal the size of the regiments on the British Establishment and to be prepared for active service, the two Irish battalions, which individually totaled 374 officers and men, required an additional ten sergeants, ten corporals, ten drummers, and 410 privates to be brought up to strength. Both groups were quickly marched to Cork, to be joined by drafts taken from the British Establishment. The Forty-fourth and Forty-eighth regiments were assigned 216 draftees apiece, but each needed another 185 men, who were later recruited in America from Virginia provincial companies not regimented. J. A. Houlding, *Fit for Service: The Training of the British Army, 1715–1795* (Oxford, 1981), 48–51.

43 REGIMENT   44 REGIMENT   45 REGIMENT

"Grenadiers, 43rd, 44th & 45th Regiments of Foot," 1751, by David Morier. Originally created to throw hand-lit grenades into enemy forts, grenadiers became the elite infantry shock troops, tall with impressive miter caps to intimidate other European armies. The 44th Regiment, part of the Irish Military Establishment, served with Braddock's army in 1755. *(The Royal Collection © 2003 Her Majesty Queen Elizabeth II. Photo: Stephen Chapman)*

38. On June 14, 1755, Washington was "seizd with violent Fevers and Pains" for a duration of nine days, remaining at Bear Camp (near present Oakton, Maryland) while Braddock's army continued on the march. The Virginian was only temporarily relieved by a dose of James's Powders. These symptoms, however, continued through July 8, when Washington finally rejoined Braddock's advance division. Following the Monongahela defeat, at which he was "very weak and low" from the illness, Washington helped organize the retreat but remained sick for at least another nine days, for a total of about five weeks. He apparently had contracted a severe case of dysentery, which recurred in the latter months of 1757. Frequent bleedings offered him no relief, with Washington explaining on March 4, 1758, that his "disorder at times [was] returning obstinately upon me." In his later "Remarks," Washington disclosed that once Fort Duquesne was seized on November 25, 1758, his health was so uncertain, having

Labels on bases: 46 REGIMENT · 47 REGIMENT · 48 REGIMENT

"been declining for many months before occasioned by an inveterate disorder in his Bowels," that he was induced to resign. *PGW, Col. Ser.*, 1: 299, 301n.7, 315–316, 319, 329–331, 352–353n.1.

39. By "Canadian French" Washington was describing the two categories of enemy troops that he encountered during the Seven Years' War: the *Compagnies franches de la Marine*, the "independent companies of marines," and the *milice*, or "militia." The *Compagnies franches* were the regular forces of Canada, organized by the department of the marine (or navy) for duty at the many colonial forts and settlements. Although the enlisted men of the *Compagnies franches* were recruited in France, most of the officers were Canadian natives. In 1754 Washington confronted officers and men of the *Compagnies franches*, including on May 28 Ensign Joseph Coulon de Villiers de Jumonville at the glen eventually to bear the latter's name, and his elder brother, Captain Louis Coulon de Villiers, at the Great Meadows on July 3–4. The second

"Grenadiers, 46th, 47th & 48th Regiments of Foot," 1751, by David Morier. The 48th Regiment, a sister unit of the 44th in Ireland, also was sent to America and Braddock's 1755 Expedition. The Redcoats made some adaptations to the American wilderness but remained targets in the forest. *(The Royal Collection © 2003 Her Majesty Queen Elizabeth II. Photo: Stephen Chapman)*

category, the *milice*, represented the citizen soldiery of Canada. The French force at the Monongahela on July 9, 1755 included seventy-two members of the *Compagnies franches*, and 146 Canadian militiamen. René Chartrand, *The French Soldier in Colonial America* (Ottawa, 1984), 9–19, 27–28; René Chartrand, *Canadian Military Heritage: Volume I, 1000–1754* (Montreal, 1993), 73–74, 96–101, 154–156.

40. Washington's memory is accurate in his description of the organization of Braddock's army, which consisted of the two regular British units, the Forty-fourth and Forty-eighth Regiments of Foot, and three Independent Companies of regulars: the Third and Fourth from New York and the Third from South Carolina. The provincial corps included nine unregimented companies of Virginians (they represented the disbanded Virginia Regiment and were not a part of the militia), a single Maryland Company, and one company from North Carolina. Not included by Washington were two additional companies, one of British regular artillery and one of sailors detached from the navy. Franklin T. Nichols, "The Organization of Braddock's Army," *William and Mary Quarterly*, 3rd. ser., 4 (April 1947): 125–136.

41. By "Champaign Countries" Washington was describing those level, unobstructed lands in northwestern Europe, where recent wars involving Britain had occurred. In 1755, the word champaign was defined as "a flat, open country" and was derived from the French *campagne*, which was a tract of open country, neither hilly nor forested. Washington may have had the War of the Austrian Succession in mind, since much of that conflict was fought by the British in the Low Countries, mainly Flanders, and in western Germany. Samuel Johnson, *A Dictionary of the English Language in which the Words are deduced from their Originals, and Illustrated in the Different Significations by Examples from the best writers* (London, 1755).

42. Braddock's progress was slowed by his cumbersome convoy, although he had already reduced the train by returning some of the light artillery and heavy British wagons to Fort Cumberland and dispersing part of the provisions and ammunition to packhorses. In a letter written at the end of June, Washington took credit for proposing the new disposition, having been asked privately by Braddock for his opinion of the expedition. The Virginian replied, "in the warmest terms I was able, to push forward; if we even did it with a small but chosen Band with such Artillery and light stores as were absolutely necessary." The remainder of

the army, he continued, could bring up the rear. The general, thirty-five miles advanced from Fort Cumberland at Little Meadows (near present Grantsville, Maryland), decided to march on Fort Duquesne with a "flying [mobile] column," a select, lightened detachment of 1,200–1,300 officers and men, which moved forward on June 19. *PGW, Col. Ser.,* 1: 321–322, 326–327n.14.

43. Thomas Dunbar (d. 1767), presumably a native of Scotland, spent in excess of three decades of service in the British army before joining Braddock in America. Following the July 9, 1755 disaster at the Monongahela and the general's death on the thirteenth, Dunbar, having missed the battle with the one-third of the army held in reserve at his camp forty miles distant, and thus the only British colonel on the expedition to remain alive or without wounds, found himself responsible for the command of all surviving forces formerly under Braddock. The colonel, however, suffering uncertain health, made the controversial decision to destroy the remaining supplies, ammunition, and even a part of the ordnance, and withdraw to Fort Cumberland. Later returned to Europe, Dunbar spent the balance of his career as lieutenant governor of the city and garrison of Gibraltar. *PGW, Col. Ser.,* 1: 264n.5; William A. Hunter, "Dunbar's March," *Cumberland County History* I, no. 1 (Summer 1984): 14–15.

44. James's Powders was a popular medicine, principally a compound of oxide of antimony and phosphate of lime, that induced a strong perspiration action to reduce high fevers and to cure inflammations; it was named for Dr. Robert James (1705–1776) of London. Braddock, an advocate of James's Powders, directed his surgeons to prescribe the medicine for Washington, to which the latter attributed his subsequent recovery. *Dictionary of National Biography,* X (London, 1908), "James, Robert," 657–658; *PGW, Col. Ser.,* 1: 319, 324n.3.

45. At the point that Braddock made the second fording of the river on July 9, the Monongahela was estimated to be between two and three hundred yards wide, but the troops found the water to be little more than knee-deep. The banks, however, were almost perpendicular and in some places twenty-four feet high. Paul E. Kopperman, "Cholmley's Batman," in *Braddock at the Monongahela* (Pittsburgh, 1977), 181.

46. A defile in the eighteenth century was "a narrow pass [and] . . . one of the greatest obstacles that can occur in the march of an army, especially if it happens to be between woods or marshes; for it . . . gives an enemy an extraordinary advantage, of either attack-

Annotation

Iroquois War Club, date unknown. Found near the field of Braddock's Defeat, this ball-headed club, carved from a single piece of maple, may have been left as a declaration of war by warriors who helped destroy the British army. The animal head on the handle is probably an Iroquois clan totem. *(Denver Art Museum Collection, Gift of Mrs. Effie Parkhill, 1951:300 © Denver Art Museum 2003)*

ing the front or rear, when they cannot come to relieve one another, because of the straightness of the passage." The "ugly" defile as referred to here impeded the lateral movement of troops, carriages and artillery, and if such a force, necessarily arrayed in dense columns with narrow fronts, were immobilized, it risked destruction in detail. Thomas Simes, *The Military Medley* (London, 1768), "defile."

47. "Hallooing" was the scalp halloo, also known as the death cry. It was a piercing shout used by warriors at the beginning of a fight as scalps were being taken, and upon their return from a raid to indicate the quantity of scalps and captives that they were bringing with them. Paul A. Wallace, *Indians in Pennsylvania* (Harrisburg, 1989), 49.

48. With the dangerous river crossing behind them, Braddock's troops, confident and almost jubilant in anticipation of victory, and having met no opposition thus far, temporarily relaxed their usual vigilance. At about one o'clock, the troops at the head of the column, having safely forded the hazardous river barrier and now well advanced into woods, found themselves to their astonishment confronting an enemy equally startled by the surprise meeting. The British instantly fired. The French commander, Captain Daniel-Hyacinthe-Marie Liénard de Beaujeu (1711–1755), in the act of deploying his men, was killed in the third volley. His deputy, Captain Jean-Daniel Dumas (1721–1792), quickly assumed control, and a powerful force of 637 warriors, 146 Canadian militia, 72 colonial marine infantry and 36 officers was immediately signaled to fan out and disappear; the men enclosed both sides of the road, flanking and ultimately almost surrounding their foe. Minutes later, the advance party of three hundred troops under Major Thomas Gage panicked and re-

treated, abandoning two six-pound field pieces, to collide with the main body of Braddock's men, which incautiously rushed forward in response to the sound of the guns. Order disintegrated as the shocked soldiers, too fearful to shoot and move against a nimble, concealed adversary, thronged together under appalling fire in a narrow corridor approximately 250 yards in length, ignoring their officers' orders and exhortations. Before abandoning the field, the Redcoats suffered in excess of eight hundred casualties in a fight of three hours against an enemy screened by trees and occupying a commanding height; the French losses were apparently less than fifty. Anderson, *Crucible of War*, 96–102.

49. Several accounts of the battle cited the danger posed by forested high ground occupied by a concealed enemy that was "scouring" the British right flank. Not long after the engagement opened, Sir John St. Clair, at the head of the column with his road builders, received a musket ball through the body. Seriously wounded, he approached Braddock and "beg'd of him for God-Sake to gain the rising ground on our Right to prevent our being Totally Surrounded"; Sir John was then rendered "insensible." Although the general subsequently made several attempts to seize the commanding hill, all of them failed. Kopperman, "Sir John St. Clair," in *Braddock at the Monongahela*, 224.

50. General Braddock remained "in the heat of action . . . greatly exposed" until being mortally wounded near the end of the engagement. His clothing had been torn by several bullets and four horses had been shot from under him; he was apparently mounting a fifth when struck by a musket ball, which passed through the back of his right arm near the shoulder, entering the side of the body downward and lodging in the right lung. Kopperman, "British A," 165, "British B," 171; Charles Hamilton, ed., *Braddock's Defeat* (Norman, Okla., 1959), 51–52n.9.

51. Robert Orme (d. 1790) was a lieutenant in the elite Coldstream Guards and principal aide-de-camp to Braddock. His considerable influence with the general caused resentment in the army, with the younger officers tending to align with Brevet Captain Orme, and the older and more senior with Colonel Sir Peter Halkett, the deputy commander. Bonded as comrades in battle, Orme held Washington in great regard; the esteem expressed was mutual. Seriously wounded in the thigh during the fighting at the Monongahela, Orme left for England several months later following his recovery and resigned from the army in 1756. *PGW, Col. Ser.*, 1: 241–242.

52. Roger Morris (1727–1794) of Yorkshire, England, was commissioned in the British army in 1745 and a decade later was

Captain Robert Orme, 1756, by Sir
Joshua Reynolds. The magnificent
portrait of Coldstream Guard Lieutenant Orme (d. 1790) was painted
on his return from America where he
had been a brevet captain as General
Braddock's principal aide and was
wounded in the thigh at the Battle of
the Monongahela. Orme had excellent
relations with another young aide,
George Washington, who also had a
high regard for the British captain.
(© *The National Gallery, London*)

Major Roger Morris, unattributed miniature. Another aide-de-camp to General Braddock, 48th Regiment Captain Morris (1727–1794) was also wounded at the Monongahela fight. He later served with Major General James Wolfe at Quebec, with the 35th and 47th regiments, married an American, settled in New York, but returned to England after the American Revolution. *(New Brunswick Museum, St. John, N.B. Webster Canadiana Collection W1182)*

selected by Braddock at Alexandria to be one of his two aides-de-camp. Also an officer of the Forty-eighth Regiment of Foot, Brevet Captain Morris was shot "through the nose" at the Monongahela. He married an American heiress in 1758 and fought at Quebec as a lieutenant colonel the following year. Morris left the army in 1764 and settled in New York, but, accused of loyalist sympathies, he and his family moved to Yorkshire, England at the close of the Revolution. *PGW, Col. Ser.*, 1: 287n.6, 334n.1–335n.1.

53. Sir Peter Halkett (*c.* 1695–1755), born in Haddingtonshire, Scotland, was colonel and commandant of the Forty-fourth Regiment of Foot. A British officer since 1717 and a combat veteran involved in the suppression of the Jacobite Rebellion in Scotland, 1745–1746, Halkett and his regiment accompanied Braddock to America. On July 9, 1755, Halkett, also serving as the provisioning officer for the army on the march to Fort Duquesne, commanded the rearguard at the Monongahela. As he calmly directed the musket fire of his men at the onset of the engagement, the colonel was

George Washington

REMEMBERS

Sir Peter Halkett, 1745, mezzotint after a portrait by Allan Ramsay. Colonel Halkett (*c.* 1695–1755) was a hero during the 1745 Scottish Rebellion and commanded the 44th Regiment during the Braddock Campaign. Halkett was killed with one of his sons early in the battle on July 9, 1755, but another son returned several years later to find and bury the remains of his father and brother lost in the wilderness. *(Fort Ligonier)*

struck by a bullet through the torso and slain. Halkett's younger son, James (*c.*1732–1755), a lieutenant in the Forty-fourth, was also killed near him. *PGW, Col. Ser.,* 1: 296n.6, 338n.5.

54. Ralph Burton (d. 1768), lieutenant colonel of the Forty-eighth Regiment of Foot, is believed to have been a native of Yorkshire, England. A major in the prestigious Horse Guards, in the fall of 1754 he transferred to the Forty-eighth Regiment as its lieutenant colonel. An efficient disciplinarian and drillmaster, Burton, although receiving "an extreme bad wound in his hip," distinguished himself in the field at the Monongahela, leading bayonet charges and valiantly attempting, but without success, to seize the dominating hill on the British right. He also tried, in vain, to rally the troops following their rout across the river. Surviving this defeat, Burton served at Louisbourg, Cape Breton Island, in 1758 and Quebec in 1759 and 1760. Promoted to major general, Burton was commander in chief of military forces in Quebec, 1764–1766, before his recall to England. *PGW, Col. Ser.,* 1: 297, 335n.1.

55. Thomas Gage (1719 or 1720–1787), born in Firle, Sussex,

GENERAL the HONble THOS GAGE
OBT 1788

"Portrait of General Thomas Gage, c. 1768, by John Singleton Copley. Then Lieutenant Colonel Gage of the 48th Regiment commanded the vanguard of Braddock's column and was criticized for his part in the British disaster at the Monongahela. He later commanded British forces in North America and was again widely condemned and then retired for his role in the early battles of the Revolutionary War. *(Yale Center for British Art, Paul Mellon Collection USA/Photo: Bridgeman Art Library)*

England, entered the army between 1736 and 1740. Assigned to Braddock as deputy commander of the Forty-eighth Regiment, Gage headed the vanguard which precipitated the engagement at the Monongahela on July 9, 1755. On this sudden encounter, a surprise to both sides, Gage formed his men and opened fire, killing the French commander, Captain Beaujeu, at the third volley. A heavy return of developing enfilade musketry quickly compelled his withdrawal and abandonment of his artillery however, as Gage was unable or unwilling to mount a bayonet charge to disrupt the enemy's lethal flanking movements. He was subsequently accused of other blunders that contributed to the disaster: Gage, supposedly reacting slowly and ineffectually, could neither prevent the disintegration of the van, which threw the troops behind him into disorder, nor seize the dominating enemy-held elevation on the right. Following two and a half hours of frustrating battle, the Englishman, slightly wounded, helped manage the panicky retreat from the field. Gage served throughout the remainder of the war, and was made commander in chief in North America in 1763. He later conducted the first engagements of the Revolution in 1775, but, much criticized, resigned and returned to England for retirement. *ANB*, 8, "Gage, Thomas," 608–610.

56. Dunbar's Camp (near present Hopwood, Pennsylvania, on the grounds of the Jumonville Christian Camp and Retreat Center) was the farthest point to which Colonel Thomas Dunbar's second division, slowly following behind the first, had marched on Braddock's Road, since the army was separated into two columns on June 19 at Little Meadows in Maryland. *PGW, Col. Ser.*, 1: 328n.20, 354n.5.

57. After his death at eight o'clock on the night of July 13, 1755, Braddock was laid to rest early the following morning. A grave was excavated on the "high road" used by the wagons not far from the Great Meadows. By interring his late commander in the middle of the road and then passing the troops, horses and all of the remaining military carriages over his resting place, Washington intended to protect the remains from discovery, scalping, and other mutilation. In 1804 (other sources variously give the years 1812, 1820, or 1824), road laborers working near the National Pike, later US Route 40, approximately one mile from the location of Fort Necessity, accidentally found a grave site, which because of the metal buttons and other artifacts they unearthed was assumed to be that of Braddock. Lee McCardell, *Ill-Starred Gen-*

General Braddock's Sash, red silk with the woven date 1709. General Braddock brought his father's 45-year-old military sash, twelve feet long and thirty inches wide, on his American campaign. The sash served its ultimate purpose when it was reportedly used to carry the mortally wounded general from the battlefield on July 9, 1755. Before his death, Braddock gave the sash and a pair of pistols to George Washington. The Virginia colonel probably wore the sash for his 1772 portrait. *(Courtesy of the Mount Vernon Ladies' Association)*

eral: Braddock of the Coldstream Guards (Pittsburgh, 1958), 272; Karl Raitz, ed., *The National Road* (Baltimore, 1996), 378–379, 443n.5; Hugh Cleland, *George Washington in the Ohio Valley* (Pittsburgh, 1955), 242, 285; Louis M. Waddell and Bruce D. Bomberger, *The French and Indian War in Pennsylvania, 1753–1763: Fortification and Struggle During the War for Empire* (Harrisburg, 1996), 12; *Niles' Weekly Register*, May 9, 1818, 79–80; Boatner, *Encyclopedia of the American Revolution*, 103.

58. On August 2, 1755, Colonel Dunbar, convinced that no further offensive action was possible, departed Fort Cumberland with the survivors of the Forty-fourth and Forty-eighth Regiments of Foot and the three Independent Companies for winter quarters in Philadelphia. This withdrawal engendered great criticism, especially from Lieutenant Governor Dinwiddie. *PGW, Col. Ser.*, 1: 342n.8.

59. On August 4, 1755, one month after Braddock's death, Lieutenant Governor Dinwiddie commissioned Washington colonel of a restructured Virginia Regiment, now to be completed, if possible, to sixteen companies. Washington officially assumed command of the unit on September 17. Brock, *Dinwiddie Papers*, II, 184–186; Elting, *Military Uniforms in America*, 20.

60. William Shirley (1694–1771), a native of Sussex, England, was successor to Braddock as British commander in chief in North America. A barrister and the governor of Massachusetts, Shirley was not a military professional, but he had gained some colonial war experience in the 1740s. Having recently planned a limited offensive strategy against the French, in February 1755 Braddock made him his deputy in America. Authorized to seize Fort Niagara and possibly to form a junction there with Braddock, Shirley and his army were unable to proceed farther than Oswego on Lake Ontario by late October 1755. Braddock's defeat and death the previous July had disrupted Shirley's original strategy, and although now the ranking officer in America, his only success was a limited offensive in Nova Scotia. His second son John (d. 1755), a captain, succumbed to fever at Oswego, and his eldest son, William Jr. (1721–1755), Braddock's secretary, had been slain at the Monongahela. As commander in chief, Shirley was visited in Boston by Washington in February 1756. Vexed by questions of rank and seniority involving provincial and regular forces, the Virginian had made his first journey to New England in part to settle these issues. Lack of accomplishment led to Shirley's recall for investigation by Parliament, but he was exonerated and made governor of the Bahamas, 1759–1767; he also was knighted. Shirley died in Massachusetts. *ANB*, "Shirley, William," 863–864.

61. By "Kings Minister" Washington was alluding to the important British government post officially titled secretary of state for the southern department. Between the years 1717 and 1768, North American provincial affairs were the responsibility of the appointee who held this position. This secretary informed and counseled the king, George II (1683–1760), on matters relevant to specific colonies or to North America in general at meetings of the Privy Council, an influential advisory body. During the period that Washington described, the second half of 1755 and early 1756, two men in succession held the secretaryship, Sir Thomas Robinson, later Baron Grantham (1695–1770), from March 23, 1754 to October 1755, and Henry Fox, later Baron Hol-

land (1705–1774), from November 14, 1755 to November 13, 1756. James Gregory and John Stevenson, *Britain in the Eighteenth Century, 1608–1620* (London, 2000), 52, 71; Alan Valentine, *The British Establishment, 1760–1784: An Eighteenth-Century Biographical Dictionary* (Norman, Okla., 1970), "Fox, James," I: 340–341; "Robinson, Thomas," II: 743–744.

62. The event in the vicinity of Fort "Vass" or Vause (present Shawsville, Virginia), said to have endangered Washington's life, probably took place in October 1756 during the colonel's inspection circuit of the backcountry defenses of the province, when he journeyed south to within five miles of the North Carolina border. The post, situated at the origin of the Roanoke River, was named for owner Ephraim Vause (b. *c.*1715), who had his dwelling fortified at his own expense in the months following Braddock's defeat. Vause's fort was captured on June 25, 1756 by a large French and Shawnee party. The incident involving Washington apparently happened when, in his words, "From Vass's I came off with a Servant and a Guide, to visit the range of forts in this county; and in less than two hours after, two men were killed along the same road." *PGW, Col. Ser.*, 3: 259–261n.2, 318, 321n.32–322n.32, 430–435n.9; Robert B. Swift, *The Mid-Appalachian Frontier: A Guide to Historic Sites of the French and Indian War* (Gettysburg, Pa., 2001), 95–96; Louis K. Koontz, *The Virginia Frontier, 1754–1763* (Baltimore, 1925), 144–145.

63. John Campbell, fourth Earl of Loudoun (1705–1782), commander in chief of the king's forces in North America, 1756–1758, was born at Loudoun Castle in Ayrshire, Scotland. He served in the British military from 1727 forward, remaining faithful to the crown during the Jacobite insurrection of 1745–1746. Dissatisfaction with Governor William Shirley as Braddock's successor as commander in chief led to the selection of Loudoun by the Duke of Cumberland on February 17, 1756. Although viewed by many in America as a martinet in the supposed manner of Braddock, Loudoun, after instilling the regular discipline, insisted that both British and provincial troops learn flexible methods of warfare suitable to the environment. Washington corresponded with Loudoun and met with him in Philadelphia on March 23, 1757, in order to request that the Virginia Regiment be brought onto the British Establishment, but Loudoun rejected his plea. Operating primarily in New York and on Cape Breton Island, Loudoun's absence of victories led to a deteriorating position both in Britain and the colonies, and he was relieved of his post in March 1758.

Annotation

Loudoun served as a British deputy commander in Portugal in 1762, and then retired to Loudoun Castle. *ANB*, 13, "Loudoun, Earl of," 941–942.

64. John Forbes (1707–1759), was a native of Dunfermline, Fifeshire, Scotland, and commander of the expedition against Fort Duquesne in 1758. Entering the army in 1735, Forbes saw combat in the War of the Austrian Succession and served on Loudoun's staff in New York in 1757. With the patronage of Sir John Ligonier (1680–1770), Cumberland's successor as commander in chief of land forces in Britain, and the approval of the new secretary of state for the southern department, William Pitt the Elder (1708–1778), Forbes was appointed brigadier general in North America in late 1757 with orders to renew the offensive in Pennsylvania. To avoid Braddock's errors, Forbes adopted the European system of constructing substantial forts approximately every forty miles as he moved on Fort Duquesne. In the event, Forbes's strategy proved a complete success, as the measured progress on his new road had allowed for the British seizure of Fort Frontenac (present Kingston, Ontario), a strategic supply depot, in August 1758, and for the conclusion of the Treaty of Easton, Pennsylvania in October, which led to negotiations with the Ohio peoples, two key factors in the triumph. The general incurred, however, the vehement objection of Washington on the selection of a new road to the Forks of the Ohio. Following the capture of Fort Duquesne on November 25, 1758, a debilitated Forbes, suffering from an unknown affliction, was carried back to Philadelphia, where he died on March 11, 1759. *ANB*, 8, "Forbes, John," 203–204.

65. The post at Loyalhanna (present Ligonier, Pennsylvania) was the most elaborate fortification project undertaken during Forbes's Pennsylvania campaign of 1758 against Fort Duquesne, and it probably was the most sophisticated fort Washington encountered between 1753 and 1758. It served as the advance base and staging area for Forbes and his army of five to six thousand troops and civilians. The installation was later named by Forbes after Sir John Ligonier. Martin West, *War for Empire in Western Pennsylvania* (Ligonier, Pa., 1993), 49, 52, 74.

66. In this passage, Washington only hints at the great controversy of the 1758 expedition on the proper military route to Fort Duquesne in which he favored Braddock's Road. Following a period of uncertainty, Forbes ignored Fort Cumberland and Braddock's Road altogether to advance across southern Pennsylvania to the Forks of the Ohio; this new road would save many miles of

travel, avoid hazardous river crossings and mislead the French as to the axis of advance. When informed of Forbes's decision, Washington was aghast; to him, the idea of another route defied military logic. Also to be remembered is that the Virginians, as with the Pennsylvanians, had other motives, since they believed that whichever road was followed to the Forks would later become the commercial highway to the west. On August 2, Washington expressed his anger on the matter, charging that "all is lost!— All is lost by Heavens!— our Enterprize Ruin[e]d; & We stop[p]ed at the Laurel Hill for this Winter." Later shown this letter, Forbes wrote privately that the "Scheme" of opposing the shorter road "was a shame" to any officer involved, and criticized Washington's conduct on the choice of routes as "no ways like a Soldier." *PGW, Col. Ser.,* 5: 360–361; Anderson, "The General Chooses a Road," *Western Pennsylvania Historical Magazine* 42, no. 2 (June 1959): 109–138, 241–258, 383–401; West, *War for Empire in Western Pennsylvania,* 52–57.

67. This incident of what is today called "friendly fire" seemingly shocked Washington into silence on the subject, at least in the known documented record, for almost three decades. At that later time he only wrote of the event in his "Remarks," with the admonition that the manuscript be returned to him or be burned. The best contemporary source is a letter from Forbes on November 17, 1758 to the commander in chief in New York, Major General James Abercromby (1706–1781), in which he briefly explained that five days earlier two hundred French and Delawares intended to strike at Loyalhanna and seize the livestock, causing him to order "500 men to give them chace with as many more to surround them, there were some killed on both sides, but unfortunately our partys fired upon each other in the dark. . . ." Immediately prior to Washington's mishap, the enemy had been driven away, but not before three prisoners were taken, one of whom, an Englishman from Lancaster County, Pennsylvania, revealed the weak state of the Fort Duquesne garrison. This intelligence led Forbes to reverse his decision of the previous day at a council of war and to renew successfully the offensive on the Forks of the Ohio. *PGW, Col. Ser.,* 6: 121n.1–123n.1.

68. George Mercer (1733–1784), field officer of the Second Virginia Regiment, was born in Stafford County, Virginia. A captain in Washington's Regiment, he fought at the Great Meadows and participated in Braddock's expedition as commander of a "Company of Carpenters." In September 1755, Washington named Mercer his aide-de-camp, and in 1757, under order of Lord Loudoun,

George Washington

REMEMBERS

George Mercer, unattributed. Virginia Lieutenant Colonel Mercer (1733–1784) was George Washington's comrade-in-arms and aide throughout the events of the French and Indian War. A twenty-one-year-old captain at Fort Necessity, Mercer went on to serve during Braddock's campaign and commanded one of the columns involved in the "friendly fire" incident of 1758. His impressive physical description of Washington in 1760 is often quoted. *(Virginia Historical Society, Richmond, Virginia)*

the commander in chief, he led two Virginia companies to defend South Carolina. For the Forbes expedition in 1758, Mercer transferred, over Washington's objection, to the newly raised Second Virginia Regiment, and was promoted lieutenant colonel. Mercer was subsequently deputy assistant quartermaster general for Maryland and Virginia, and after the war represented the Ohio Company in London. Alfred P. James, "George Mercer, of the Ohio Company: A Study in Frustration, Part I: In America, 1733–1763," *The Western Pennsylvania Historical Magazine* 46, no. 1 (January 1963): 1–43; James, "George Mercer, of the Ohio Company: A Study of Frustration, Part II: Voluntary Exile, 1763–1764," Ibid. 46, no. 2 (April 1963): 141–183.

69. Washington's orderly book for November 13, 1758 contained the entry, "A Return to be givin in this Evening at 7 o clock of the Number of Men Killd and wounded and missing in the Skirmish last night. . . ," but this casualty list has not been found. His recollection in the "Remarks" that a single officer and "several privates" were slain "and many wounded" is lower than some other estimates, but may exclude losses suffered in the earlier fire-

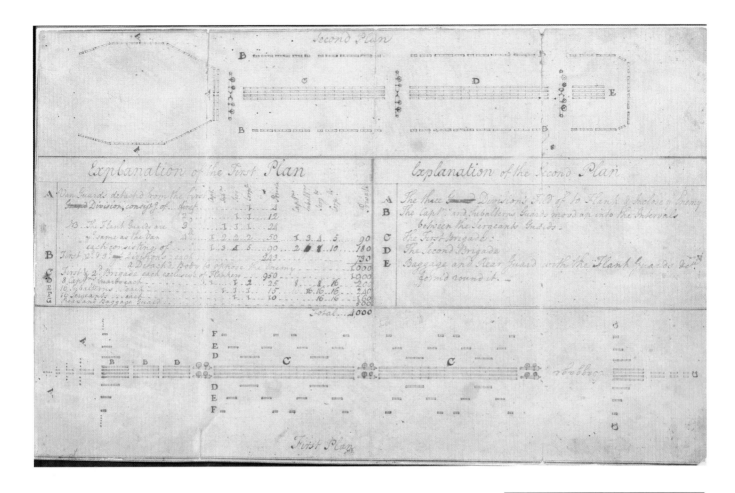

fight with the enemy. Lacking the November 13 return, the closest official account of the accident was sent from Loyalhanna to General Abercromby by Forbes on November 17, which stated, "we lost two officers and 38 private kill'd or missing." *PGW, Col. Ser.*, 6: 121n.1–123n.1; Alfred P. James, *Writings of General John Forbes Relating to his Service in North America* (Menasha, Wis., 1938), 255.

70. In the face of an overwhelming British force, the vastly outnumbered French decided to raze Fort Duquesne by detonating a mine and to evacuate the garrison to safety on the night of November 24. The commandant of Fort Duquesne since November 1756, Captain François Le Marchand-Marie, de Ligneris (1703–1760), ordered the artillery and munitions to be placed in bateaux, in addition to all prisoners, and sent down the Ohio River. They apparently retreated to Fort de l'Assumption (present Metropolis, Illinois) on the north side of the river in *les pays des Illinois*, "the Illinois Country," the immense tract of French territory located south of Lake Michigan and approximately bordered by the Wabash, Illinois, and Mississippi rivers. On November 25, the British occupied the site of Fort Duquesne, which Forbes renamed "Pittsburgh" in honor of William Pitt. Proved wrong in his prognosis of disaster, Washington wrote that the capture of

"Plan of a Line of March and Order of Battle," 8 October, 1758, by George Washington. Asked by commanding General John Forbes for suggestions on how to advance the army toward Fort Duquesne, Colonel Washington drew up a detailed plan describing how to protect a marching column in the woods and to effectively meet an attacking enemy. No one in the army had more experience fighting the French and Indians and Washington's suggestions were agreed to by General Forbes. *(The Pierpoint Morgan Library, New York, MA 878. Photo: Joseph Zehavi)*

Fort Duquesne was a "great surprise to the whole army," and due only to the weakness of the enemy.

Despite Washington's vociferous resistance to the building of the Forbes Road, the knowledge, training and insight he gained in 1758 completed his early education as a soldier. In emulation of Forbes and others, he had become a professional officer, learning the military art equivalent to that of a colonel in the British army, since his First Virginia Regiment was probably comparable to any corresponding regular king's battalion. From Forbes, Washington belatedly appreciated that to succeed in campaigns, even war, battlefield victories were not always essential, and that by patiently maintaining the army and its objectives, tactical defeats could be overcome. John Forbes gained no actual triumphs in the field, yet achieved his goal of capturing Fort Duquesne. The general, although greatly disappointed in the behavior of Washington, also recognized his abilities, and retained sufficient confidence to seek the Virginian's advice and to appoint him a brevet brigadier for the final advance. Eric Hinderaker, *Elusive Empires: Constructing Colonialism in the Ohio Valley: 1673–1800* (Cambridge, 1997), 143–144; *PGW, Col. Ser.*, 6: 158; James, *Writings of Forbes*, 262–267; Anderson, *Crucible of War*, 289–293, 749n.10.

71. This letter, written and dated from Fort Loudoun at Winchester on December 31, 1758, was entitled "The humble Address of the Officers of the Virginia Regiment." Twenty-seven officers signed the missive, imploring Washington to remain in the military for an additional year to complete the victory over the French. *PGW, Col. Ser.*, 6: 178–180.

72. Washington's response to his officers' "Address" was sent from Mount Vernon on January 10, 1759. In it, he thanked them for their service, but said nothing of the two reasons cited in the "Remarks," the capture of Fort Duquesne and a long illness, for his resignation, only offering ambiguously that he had "for some years [operated] under uncommon difficulties, which few were throughly acquainted with." Washington also made no comment on the officers' request that he continue another year in the army, and concluded by expressing his high regard for them, with the promise to assist them when possible in the future. *PGW, Col. Ser.*, 6: 186–187.

73. Washington's comment refers to this passage by Humphreys: "*After some years, he [Washington] gave up planting tobacco & went altogether into the farming business. Before the [Revolutionary] war he raised [   ] bushels of wheat, in one year.*" Zagarri, *Humphreys' "Life of General Washington,"* 24.

74. Washington's comment refers to this passage by Humphreys: "*When he [Washington] became a citizen, he had the uncommon felicity to find that his native State was among the most zealous in doing justice to his merits, & that stronger demonstrations of affectional esteem (if possible) were given by the citizens in his neighbourhood, than by any other description of men of the Continent.*" Zagarri, *Humphreys' "Life of General Washington,"* 33.

Thomas Mifflin (1744–1800), revolutionary general and Pennsylvania politician, was born in Philadelphia. The letter to which Washington referred in his "Remarks" was apparently the one sent by Mifflin, at the time president of Congress, on December 28, 1783, which proposed that a financial remuneration be arranged by that legislative body in recompense for the many public services rendered by the retiring general. The proposed monetary awards were never authorized, probably due to Washington's opposition. *ANB*, 15, "Mifflin, Thomas," 440–441; *PGW, Confederation Series*, 1: 25, 42.

With the close of the Revolution, one of Washington's first priorities as a civilian in 1784 was to establish a public company to enhance the navigation of the Upper Potomac River and connect it to the watershed of the Ohio Valley, an interest he harbored for more than a decade. The Potomac River and James River Companies were consequently authorized by the state of Virginia in January 1785. That same date, Washington was informed of the additional action of the legislature, which awarded him fifty shares in the Potomac River Company and one hundred in the James River Company. Vexed by what he saw as a predicament, Washington contacted several friends and associates for their advice on the matter and the appropriate manner in which to respond. On October 29, 1785, he officially rejected the offer, with the request that it be transferred "to objects of a public nature," to which the legislators agreed. *PGW, Conf. Ser.*, 2: 86–89, 256–257n.1, 261.

75. Washington's comment refers to this passage by Humphreys: "*He [Washington] keeps a pack of hounds, & in the season indulges himself with hunting once in a week, at which diversion the gentlemen of Alexandria often assist.*" Zagarri, *Humphreys' "Life of General Washington,"* 37.

76. Washington's comment refers to this passage by Humphreys: "*Agriculture is the favorite employment of General Washington, in which he wishes to pass the remainder of his days. To acquire practical knowledge, he corresponds with Mr Arthur Young who has written so sensibly on the subject.*" Zagarri, *Humphreys' "Life of General Washington,"* 37.

Arthur Young (1741–1820), a noted agricultural expert, was born in London, England and became a prolific writer, achieving an international reputation. Pro-American and an admirer of Washington, in 1801 he published in London *Letters from His Excellency General Washington to Arthur Young, Esq., F. R. S. DNB*, XXI, "Young, Arthur," 1272–1278; *PGW, Conf. Ser.*, 3: 499.

77. Washington's comment refers to this passage by Humphreys: "*[In addition to Young he also corresponds] with many agricultural gentlemen in this Country; and as improvement is known to be his passion, he receives envoys of rare seeds & results of new projects, from every quarter. He also makes copious Notes in writing relative to his own experiments the state of the seasons, nature of soils, effect of different kinds of manure & everything that can throw light on the farming business.*" Zagarri, *Humphreys' "Life of General Washington,"* 37.

George Washington

REMEMBERS

Part II

George Washington, 1787, by Charles Willson Peale. Artist Peale, a close friend of George Washington, coaxed his painter-shy subject to sit for seven portraits. This likeness, painted in Philadelphia during the 1787 Constitutional Convention, captures the 55-year-old hero at the time he wrote the "Remarks," recalling his role in the French and Indian War. *(Courtesy of the Pennsylvania Academy of the Fine Arts, Philadelphia; Bequest of Mrs. Sarah Harrison, The Joseph Harrison, Jr. Collection)*

Don Higginbotham
University of North Carolina at
Chapel Hill

Young Washington One

AMBITION, ACCOMPLISHMENT, AND ACCLAIM

I T WOULD be hard to exaggerate the significance of the French and Indian War in the life and fortunes of George Washington. His role in that conflict indicates at least three things worthy of examination. It reveals an exceedingly ambitious man, who, along with some failures and disappointments, accomplished a great deal while in uniform, and who emerged a well-known and highly respected figure in colonial America and in Britain. (His visibility, although not acclaim, extended to France.) These three factors do much to explain the future trajectory of Washington's public life. As a Virginia military hero, Washington launched his postwar career in public service by being elected to the Virginia House of Burgesses. He would hardly be the last soldier in this country to use his wartime accomplishments as a vehicle to other positions of authority. Even though Washington, subsequent to his time in arms in the 1750s, spent seventeen years in the legislature of the Old Dominion, his performance in the colonial assembly fails to explain his opportunity to perform on a larger stage that became the American Revolution. He was, to be sure, a member of the gentry, a niche enhanced by an economically profitable marriage, but he never became a member of the inner circle of power in the Burgesses, on a par with the Randolphs, Robinsons, Lees, Carters, and other lordly clans.

One must ask then, why was he elected by his fellow members

to the First and Second Continental Congresses, in 1774 and 1775 respectively, and on both occasions with more votes than most other members of the Virginia delegations sent to Philadelphia? Washington, as we will see later, was a highly visible man, more experienced in military affairs than perhaps any American, except for several former British officers who had recently retired from the king's service and settled in the colonies. In 1774, following the passage of Parliament's harsh Coercive Acts, in response to the Boston Tea Party, the possibility of armed conflict confronted leaders of the American resistance. Virginians, before Lexington and Concord, had sought Washington's assistance in reorganizing and training their county militias.[1] Indeed, as early as the Townshend Crisis of 1767–1770, Washington had acknowledged that Americans might have to resort to force to defend their liberties.

Washington learned long before adulthood that families striving for greater recognition and rewards might find them from wearing a uniform. He always remembered that his oldest half-brother Lawrence had sought the friendship and favor of Virginia's Governor William Gooch, who in 1740 commanded thirty-six companies of men raised in the colonies, known as Gooch's American Foot, to participate in a British military and naval expedition against the Spanish in the Caribbean. Gooch appointed Lawrence Washington as the senior captain of the six Virginia companies. The Caribbean venture, highlighted by an unsuccessful attack on the fortress at Cartagena, ended in failure for Anglo-provincial forces, but not before Lawrence had won the favor of Vice Admiral Edward Vernon, who headed the expedition. Lawrence, who named his estate Mount Vernon after the admiral, had also attracted the attention of General Thomas Wentworth, who commanded the British land forces at Cartagena, and who, following the campaign, aided Lawrence as a now-retired regular officer to win army half pay for life. After Lawrence returned to Virginia, Gooch continued to bestow upon the young veteran patronage and preferment. He selected him as a county justice of the peace and named him to the post of Adjutant General of the Militia of Virginia, which provided a salary second only to the governor's. Lawrence further rooted himself more firmly in the upper levels of the Virginia aristocracy by marrying Ann Fairfax, daughter of Colonel William Fairfax, a former British officer. In Virginia, Colonel Fairfax became one of the most influential members of the royal council and acted as the principal business agent for his cousin Thomas, Sixth Lord

Admiral Edward Vernon, *c*.1753, by Thomas Gainsborough. Admiral Vernon (1684–1757) was immortalized for Americans as the inspiration for the name of the Mount Vernon Plantation. George Washington's older half-brother Lawrence, a veteran of the 1740 War of Jenkins's Ear, honored his former commander by renaming his Potomac River estate on Little Hunting Creek. *(By Courtesy of the National Portrait Gallery, London)*

Fairfax, proprietor of the colony's vast Northern Neck.

Although it would be risky to contend that Washington consciously sought to advance his public and private fortunes in the exact order and manner that Lawrence had done, the close parallels make doing so a great temptation. We have only to look at Washington's relationships with another governor of Virginia, Robert Dinwiddie, with another senior British military man, Edward Braddock (and there would be other British generals after Braddock), with another woman, Martha Dandridge Custis, who became his wife, and with another family. But in this case it was the same family that supported Lawrence, the Fairfaxes, although of course Washington did not marry into that clan. He too saw the Fairfaxes as a key to his future standing in the Old Dominion.

Robert Dinwiddie, the new Virginia chief executive, arrived in the colony in the fall of 1751, just a matter of days or a few weeks after George and his half-brother Lawrence took ship for the island of Barbados in the West Indies. George traveled as a companion and possible caregiver for Lawrence, who sought a healthier climate to arrest his failing health from tuberculosis. Dinwiddie, veteran crown civil servant, had earlier held administrative posts in Virginia and in Barbados and retained a close friendship with a Barbadian planter and merchant, Gedney Clark, who agreed to be the principal host of the Washington brothers. Still another valuable link for Washington in the chain of relationships was the fact that Dinwiddie, Clark, and Colonel Fairfax had known one another for many years. Unfortunately, the West Indian trip did not aid Lawrence, whose health continued to decline. Washington returned to Virginia ahead of his half-brother as Lawrence tried the island of Bermuda in a final effort to regain his health before he too returned home, barely in time to set his affairs in order before dying in 1752.

From the moment that Washington arrived in Williamsburg with letters from Clark and others for Dinwiddie—the governor asked the young man to stay for dinner—the lives of the two men were closely intertwined until Dinwiddie departed from Virginia in 1758. Dinwiddie obviously found Washington earnest, able, and physically imposing. Various contemporaries described the young Washington as strong and muscular, displaying feats of skill. Jefferson called Washington the most graceful equestrian of his generation. If Dinwiddie consequently did numerous things to advance Washington in the public sector out of respect for the

Robert Dinwiddie, c.1760–1765, unattributed. The 60-year-old Scot (1692–1770) came to Virginia and served as Lieutenant Governor (1751–1758) during the frontier conflict with the French and Indians. Described as having the "face of a longtime tax collector," Dinwiddie launched the military career of George Washington but later clashed with the impetuous young colonel over support for the Virginia troops. *(By Courtesy of the National Portrait Gallery, London)*

talented young man, he assuredly had a second motive as well: the governor needed the political backing of Colonel Fairfax, who had become president of the Virginia council, and who appeared almost as committed to Washington as he had been to Lawrence, the colonel's deceased son-in-law. Though relatively few of their letters have survived, it is apparent that the colonel and his protégé corresponded with some regularity during the following years as Fairfax and Dinwiddie jointly took every opportunity to advance Washington's ambitions for a military career. Washington undoubtedly had himself foremost in mind when he wrote in later years of "a natural fondness of Military parade" on the part "of able bodied young Men between the Age of 18 and 25." He might have added from his own earlier experience that the best method of achieving that goal was through securing a patron or, as he phrased it in the language of the time, an "interest."[2] As he confided to his younger brother "Jack," John Augustine, Colonel Fairfax was their patron. The brothers had every incentive to "live in perfect Harmony" with Fairfax and his family "as it is in their power to be very serviceable upon many occasion's to us as young beginner's."[3]

Thanks to Dinwiddie, with the approval of Fairfax and other members of the Council, Washington's military career in Virginia began by following the course of Lawrence's, with an appointment as a militia administrator. Lawrence, however, started as adjutant for the entire colony; but on Lawrence's death, Dinwiddie split the duties by creating several military districts, with an adjutant for each. In 1752, twenty-one-year-old Washington became adjutant for the southern district, and a short time later, at his request he was switched to the northern district.[4]

The following year Washington's talents, ambitions, and "interest" combined to provide him with an incredible adventure, which was also dangerous and arduous. The French, rivals with Britain for the Ohio Valley, sent major exploring parties into this region claimed by both European powers, one that the colony of Virginia's Ohio Company had sought to develop by selling its land grants in that area to investors and settlers. Dinwiddie himself was a major shareholder and so had been the late Lawrence Washington. Soon after Dinwiddie indicated his intention to send an emissary to warn the French to give up their scheme of establishing a post at the juncture of the Monongahela and the Allegheny with the Ohio River and to withdraw from their recently constructed string of forts stretching south from

Lake Erie, Washington volunteered for the mission. Presumably he rode to Williamsburg to offer his services. It makes sense to speculate that Colonel Fairfax, who heard Dinwiddie propose the undertaking to his Council, had tipped off Washington and urged him to appear before the governor. And Dinwiddie chose the twenty-two-year-old volunteer, after consulting with his Council.[5]

Here the young man first walked onto the pages of history. His journey and back in the fall and early winter of 1753–1754 covered several hundred miles and took two and a half months. He and his small party of frontiersmen and Indians encountered almost every imaginable wilderness hazard, including extreme exposure and near death. The French commandant at Fort de la Rivière au Boeuf near Lake Erie charmed his guests but rejected Dinwiddie's injunction. Even so, Washington learned much from his contacts with various Indian tribes and French soldiers and saw firsthand the great potential of the sprawling Appalachian landscape. At Dinwiddie's request, Washington wrote an account of his adventures in the Ohio Country. Published on both sides of the Atlantic, it first introduced him to a wide audience. At home, his stature grew as the Virginia General Assembly praised him for his difficult undertaking by awarding him £50. Dinwiddie kept him on the payroll of the colony.

The governor had further plans of a military nature for the young man, who must have quite openly conveyed his eagerness to take up arms. In response to the French menace, Dinwiddie began to recruit a regiment rather than resort to an all-militia force.

Washington confided to Richard Corbin, an influential councillor, that he wished to be appointed lieutenant colonel and second in command. If Washington seemed brash in view of his tender twenty-two years and inexperience, he remained ever mindful of his important connections. Dinwiddie appointed him, only to find that Washington complained that his lieutenant-colonel's salary was too low; but once more William Fairfax exerted himself, assuring the young man that the remuneration of the officers of what became known as the Virginia Regiment would be increased as soon as possible.

With two companies, Washington set off to protect a contingent of Virginians constructing a warehouse for the Ohio Company at the forks of the Ohio. Once again, accounts of his activities would reach as far as the council chambers of Europe. Soon after he learned that the French had gained possession of that strategic

Young Washington

AMBITION,
ACCOMPLISHMENT,
AND ACCLAIM

location, Washington surprised a French party advancing in his direction. He announced triumphantly to Dinwiddie that in fifteen minutes his men had killed ten, including Ensign Jumonville, the commander, while he suffered only one fatality. Quite possibly Jumonville's objective was, like Washington's journey to Fort de la Rivière au Boeuf, intended only to warn a competing power to get out of a disputed region. Whatever the truth, Washington harbored no second thoughts about his heady experience: he "was exposed to & received all the Enemy's fire." He had "heard Bulletts whistle and . . . there was something charming in the sound," he exclaimed to his brother Jack.[6]

Things were surely breaking Washington's way. Basking in the publicity of his Ohio Country excursion, he had won decisively in a small but much heralded battle.

He was on a roll, so to speak. He garnered applause in Williamsburg and further visibility in London when a copy of his letter to Jack appeared in the *London Magazine*, where King George II read the account. And now Washington became the

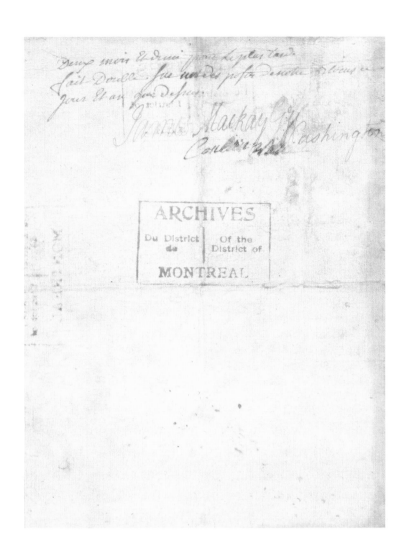

ranking officer of the Virginia Regiment because his former superior, Colonel Joshua Fry, had died.

Washington had gained such a positive reputation that he could now weather any blip on his record, provided it amounted to no more than a blip. That is exactly what happened. After erecting a stockade, Fort Necessity, at the Great Meadows, near the site of his victory over Jumonville, Washington received word that French reinforcements had reached Fort Duquesne and that 1,200 enemy regulars and Indians, out to avenge Jumonville's fall, bore down upon his miniscule body of Virginians. Hastily pulling back his advance elements to Fort Necessity, he found it too late for a general withdrawal. His own tribal allies abandoned him, and his supplies were low. After enduring a day-long siege in a steady rain, he surrendered, on a date he never forgot: July 3, 1754.

Despite his capitulation, he emerged with his reputation relatively unscathed. He himself felt he had done his best under the circumstances, and his adversaries permitted him to march away with the honors of war. Dinwiddie and his other Virginia friends in high places protected him from criticism. They believed him when he said he had done all he could. They even absolved him of blame for signing at Fort Necessity articles of surrender in which he acknowledged "*l'assassin*" of Jumonville. The commander of the French force, a brother of Jumonville, had insisted on the language, which the Gallic officer later said was a confession to the murder of Jumonville at the Great Meadows. But his Williamsburg backers and much of London officialdom claimed that Washington had signed the articles under duress, and he had not understood the meaning of the French word in question. The matter became a kind of propaganda war in Paris, London, and Williamsburg.

For better or worse, Washington always seemed to be in the limelight. He resigned his commission as commander of the Virginia Regiment over seniority issues that had arisen when British officers balked at taking orders from colonials, for whom they often displayed ill-disguised disdain. The decision to reduce provincial officers—in Washington's case, from colonel to captain—was made by Governor Horatio Sharpe of Maryland, who had recently acquired a crown commission, acting with the approval of Governors Dinwiddie and Arthur Dobbs of North Carolina. But when Sharpe's plans to direct an expedition to oust the French from the interior failed to materialize, Washington looked for a new opportunity as a soldier that would not conflict with his honor after being demoted. He had no desire "to leave the military line," he informed Colonel William Fitzhugh, a prominent Stafford County burgess, who had served with Lawrence in the Cartagena campaign; his "inclinations" were still "strongly bent to arms."[7]

Washington's solution came when British General Edward Braddock, with two regiments of redcoats, landed at Alexandria, Virginia, in February, 1755 and prepared to move against the French at Fort Duquesne. Washington masked his ambitions by claiming that Braddock, in need of scouts and others familiar with the region, had requested his services. Washington added that he accepted the offer to serve as a volunteer aide only because his "sole motive" was "the laudable desire of serving my country."[8] In fact, Washington had advanced his own ambitions, congratulating Braddock on his "safe arrival" and indicating his availability as one who knew the wilderness and the ways of Indians. Once again, the best insight into Washington's actual motives comes from his letters to his brother Jack. This correspondence

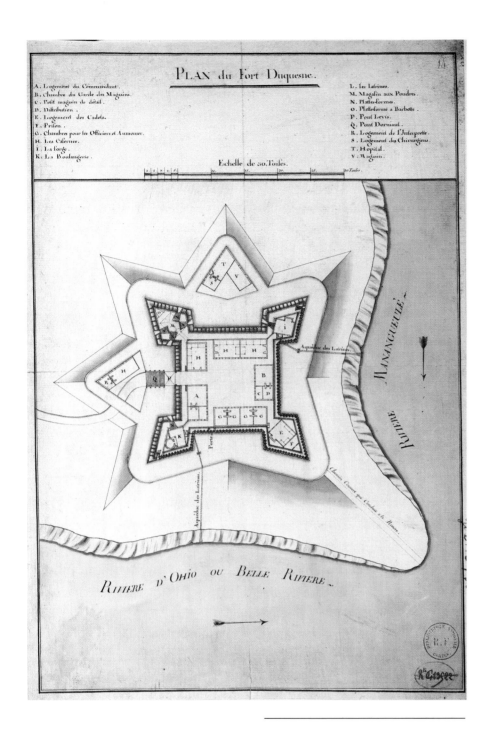

Young Washington

AMBITION,
ACCOMPLISHMENT,
AND ACCLAIM

"Plan of Fort Duquesne," *c.*1754–1758.
The French won the race to the Forks
of the Ohio in 1754 and built the first
substantial fort on the point. Frontier
Fort Duquesne, named for the Marquis de Duquesne, Governor of New
France, was declared not "worth a
straw" but defied all British attempts
to capture it for more than four years.
*(Cliché Bibliothèque nationale de
France, Paris)*

reveals his desire to increase his "knowledge in the Military Art" and to further his "Fortune in the Military way."[9]

The Braddock expedition brought Washington both of his objectives, but hardly in the manner he had desired. For the first time, he served with a British army. He carefully observed its methods and procedures, and he had lengthy conversations with junior and field grade officers about the military art. He developed a close relationship with Captain Robert Orme, the general's senior aide, and he enjoyed cordial ties with Colonel Thomas Gage, who led the army's advance party. It is also quite probable that he became well acquainted with Captains Charles Lee and Horatio Gates, competent officers who in later years left the army and settled in the Shenandoah Valley of Virginia. Washington made successful efforts to spend time with General Braddock himself, conversations that the young Virginia volunteer would remember for a lifetime.

Moreover, the Battle of the Monongahela, on July 9, gave the volunteer aide more than enough of the combat experience he had sought. The French and Indian assault on the flanks of Braddock's extended column brought disaster to British arms and near death to Washington, who displayed bravery and heroism. "I luckily escaped with[ou]t a wound," he assured his mother, "tho' I had four Bullets through my Coat, and two Horses shot under me."[10] He believed he had done all that he could to aid in rallying the disorganized regulars, and he praised the companies of Virginia troops for standing bravely against great odds. "They behavd like Men, and died like Soldiers," whereas the redcoats displayed "dastardly behavior"; they acted like "Sheep pursued by dogs; and it was impossible to rally them."[11]

Although Washington's view of the catastrophe may well have been largely true, the point worth stressing is that he made a concerted effort to make it the accepted version in Virginia. He wrote letters similar to the one to his mother to other parties. Most important, he wasted no time in dispatching one to Governor Dinwiddie. In the Old Dominion, Washington and the other surviving Virginians became heroes. They were hailed as "Our Brave Blues" because they wore blue coats with red facings. Stories had it that the dying Braddock praised Washington and his "dear Blues" and cursed the sight of his cowardly redcoats. At least one British participant echoed Washington's praise of the Virginians. Colonel Fairfax, Washington's powerful mentor, exclaimed to him that his "safe Return" gave "uncommon Joy" to all "true Lovers of Heroick virtue." Dinwiddie dispatched copies of Washington's missive to Britain, several of which survive today in the United Kingdom. In London, the *Gentlemen's Magazine* echoed various accounts in the British press when it extolled the courage of the Virginians and castigated the regulars' conduct. Washington's role in the battle and retreat also elicited the praise of his Uncle Joseph Ball, a Londoner, who concluded his letter to his nephew by saying, "Go on as you have begun; and God prosper you."[12]

With Braddock's army decimated and its shattered remains under Colonel Thomas Dunbar limping to Philadelphia, Virginia would have to defend its own frontiers from the Gallic and Indian host, and Washington, its hero, again became the man of the hour. Dinwiddie authorized a new Virginia Regiment and the recently demoted colonel, with his rank restored, received the command. At only twenty-three he had already experienced a most eventful young adulthood—a trip to Barbados, an appointment as militia adjutant, a diplomatic mission to the Ohio Valley, and several military engagements against the French: at Jumonville Glen, at Fort Necessity, and at the Monongahela with Braddock.

The next three years were anything but exciting and gratifying to the youthful officer who had spoken of the thrill of battle after defeating Ensign Jumonville.

His regiment never reached its manpower goals as enlistments lagged and he resorted to drafts from unhappy militiamen. He remained consistently short of everything necessary for protecting the backcountry settlers and beating off Indian incursions. Many Virginians saw the war as oppressive in its demands upon them, fought in the judgment of some to fulfill the ambitious western schemes of the Ohio Company and other land speculators.[13] Few if any of Washington's travails resulted from personal errors or misdeeds. Possibly an older, stoical regimental commander might have displayed more tact. Washington, however, often blamed others, especially Governor Dinwiddie and the Council, when in fact most of the colonel's problems resulted from inadequate political machinery, lack of financial resources, and difficulties of cooperation and coordination involving the individual colonies and Britain's own antiquated war machinery for waging campaigns three thousand miles from London.

His legitimate concerns and his unfair accusations against Williamsburg officialdom notwithstanding, Washington the soldier made the most of his circumstances and performed impressively. He imparted a sense of professionalism to the core of his

Young Washington

AMBITION,

ACCOMPLISHMENT,

AND ACCLAIM

regimental officers and enlisted men (as opposed to the wayward militia). He instructed his field officers and company captains to be firm but fair to their men, which included giving legitimate attention to their concerns and grievances. If they should deal sternly with disobedience, his subordinates should be especially severe in handling those who mistreated the civilian population. Officers were to keep careful records of troop strength and supplies and equipment, just as they were to read European military literature, employ British methods of marching and drilling, stress neatness in appearance, and attire their men in uniforms if at all possible. One has to be impressed in reading Washington's general orders over his three-year period as colonel of the Virginia Regiment. They were clear, crisp, and comprehensive, as if they had been issued by a first-rate officer in the king's army.[14]

Washington and his officers had as their objective—in making the military "your profession," as their colonel phrased it—being taken into the British regular establishment.[15] His officers proudly claimed in a "Memorial" designed to assist Washington in this quest that they were "the first in arms, of any Troops" in America during the current war. They were not to be confused with militia but rather were soldiers seasoned by "many bloody" encounters with the enemy.[16] This quest involved Washington with a succession of British commanders. Initially, he sought only regular status for himself when he broached the subject to Braddock, who informed Washington that he could issue commissions at no higher rank than captain, a status unacceptable to the sensitive young Virginian. But by 1756 his ambitions extended to the Virginia Regiment as well and led him to exertions that, though failing, gave him the opportunity to see an expansive slice of America that extended far north of the Old Dominion. That year he traveled up the Atlantic coast to Boston, where he made his appeal to Governor William Shirley of Massachusetts, who served temporarily as British commander in chief. Though Shirley felt he lacked the authority to grant regular status to Washington and his troops, he remarked to Governor Sharpe that he knew of "no Provincial officer upon the Continent as deserving of a high position" as Washington.[17] Ever a persistent, determined man, Washington set out again the following year, this time to Philadelphia, to present his case to Shirley's successor, John Campbell, Lord Loudoun, who hardly gave a priority to Washington's desire to play a major part in a campaign against Fort Duquesne. The new commander in chief chose to focus on immediate operations against Canada, not the Ohio Valley.

John Campbell, fourth earl of Loudoun, 1754, by Allan Ramsay. Scottish born Lord Loudoun (1705–1782) was an energetic and professional commander in chief of the king's forces in North America (1756–1758). Arrogant toward Americans, he rejected Colonel Washington's request that the provincial Virginia regiment be made regular royal troops. *(Fort Ligonier)*

Although denied again his efforts for a colonel's commission and for a royalized regiment, Washington continued to impress his British superiors. Loudoun did Washington a personal favor, and Washington, in asking that favor of His Lordship, paid a debt to the memory of Colonel William Fairfax, who had recently died.[18] At least partly owing to Washington's warm recommendation, Loudoun "very kindly" received Colonel Fairfax's young son William Henry and "willingly consented" to "Billy's" purchasing an ensign's commission.[19]

Although later Washington was saddened to learn of "Billy's" death along with that of General James Wolfe on the Plains of Abraham at Quebec, Washington's own prospects for greater recognition, but not promotion, brightened in 1758 with the appointment of General John Forbes to launch a campaign against Fort Duquesne. William Pitt, the energetic new head of the ministry, showed his determination to turn the war in America in a more positive direction following a string of setbacks since Braddock's fiasco. Pitt's selection of the able Forbes as part of a fresh team of military leadership, placing talent above seniority, included bringing attention back to the Ohio Valley and the Southern colonies. Part of the good news for Virginia was Pitt's agreeing to provide American legislatures with handsome financial subsidies, a commitment that led the Virginia lawmakers to provide bounties to increase the ranks of Washington's depleted Virginia Regiment and to raise a 2d Virginia Regiment under William Byrd III, a councillor and member of a tidewater first family. Moreover, "the Great Commoner" rectified a long-standing grievance of provincial officers. Virginia's Colonels Washington and Byrd, as well as other American field officers, would now be junior in standing only to redcoats of their own rank and higher. Probably no American officer had displayed more sensitivity on this issue than Colonel Washington, who twice had encountered British captains who had been contemptuous of his higher rank.

Just as Washington had ardently sought the favor of every British commander he had served under, so now he launched an effort to ingratiate himself with the recently promoted Forbes, a fifty-year-old Scot, probably the most talented general Washington encountered in the war. The Virginian dashed off entreaties to Colonel Thomas Gage and General John Stanwix to mention his name favorably to Forbes. Not that he sought preferential treatment, he informed Stanwix; he wished merely to "be distinguished . . . from the *common run*" or "motley herd" of provincial officers. To Gage, his fellow campaigner with Braddock, Washington became quite specific: Forbes should know that he had been "much longer in the Service than any provincial officer in America."[20] Although Forbes seems to have responded positively to reports on Washington and to his own initial encounters with the Virginia colonel, their relationship temporarily cooled because Forbes rejected Washington's strenuous arguments against proceeding toward the French stronghold by moving westward from Raystown, Pennsylvania rather than by advancing along Braddock's old road some miles to the south. In fact, Washington and Colonel Byrd, to Forbes's great distress, were downright antagonistic and conveyed their feelings to their Williamsburg cronies, asserting that Forbes had been hoodwinked by Pennsylvania authorities who wished to use the Raystown route as the means to monopolize the Ohio Valley trade—to the exclusion of Virginians—in the postwar years.

Once the army moved forward, Forbes put his feelings aside and encouraged Washington to express his views on how to advance and guard the column from Braddock's mistakes. Washington, the only provincial to head a forward division, missed out on any major engagements with the outnumbered French, who saw their Indian allies depart and consequently abandoned and burned Fort Duquesne.

With the war on the Virginia frontier at an end and with no new martial challenges or hopes for a British commission, Washington concluded the year 1758 by resigning his post. There is every reason to believe that, in making his decision, he must have reflected on his last five years, all spent in the military service of his "country," as he called Virginia. In his subsequent written reminiscences, there is no evidence that he ever acknowledged his partisanship in dealing with Governor Dinwiddie and General Forbes, a trait of denying mistakes and wrongdoing that persisted to his death. The former had given him his opportunities for public recognition, suffering through his outbursts of temper, and the latter had put up with his carping while teaching him a good deal about soldiering and giving him valuable opportunities in command. His relations with those worthies revealed his ardent ambitions, as had his dealings with Sharpe, Braddock, Shirley, and Loudoun. And so had his courting the favor of Colonel William Fairfax. Washington no longer needed Virginia benefactors such as Fairfax, now dead, and Dinwiddie, who had been replaced as governor of the Old Dominion. Whatever the reservations of several of them about his occasional unseemly behavior, they all rec-

Young Washington

AMBITION,

ACCOMPLISHMENT,

AND ACCLAIM

ognized his determination, hard work, and abilities. And so had other British military men and his own subordinates in the Virginia Regiment. His departure elicited a "humble Address from the Officers," sadly "Affected with loss of such an excellent Commander, such a sincere Friend, and so affable a Companion."[21]

Like Lawrence Washington, the younger Washington had left the service, entered the political world—having been elected to the House of Burgesses in 1758—and married. Martha Dandridge Custis was an attractive widow with two young children and substantial wealth at her disposal, both her dower rights and the benefits of her offsprings' inheritance. Washington now also had more-than-average resources of his own, which included the renting of Mount Vernon, which a short time later came into his possession owing to the death of Lawrence's widow and of their only surviving child.

Washington was highly respected and visible. The citizens of Winchester in Frederick County, where he had made his military headquarters for most of the war, had not only elected him to the House of Burgesses but had named a street for him, the first of countless such forms of honor and recognition in his lifetime. It is doubtful that he thought of ever bearing arms again, even though he tried unsuccessfully to buy statue busts of six famous generals and elected to pose in 1772 for his first known portrait, limned by the artist Charles Willson Peale, wearing his old military uniform. In any event, the Reverend Samuel Davies, the most influential Presbyterian minister in the Old Dominion, had preached what proved to be a prophetic sermon during the late conflict with France. Davies asserted that Washington's "uncommon bravery, conduct, and knowledge in the art of war, at his age, is superior to what I ever read of; and he seems as if appointed by Providence to be hereafter, the protector and deliver of his country." It was a prediction that the printer of a Virginia newspaper brought to the attention of its readers during the dark days of the Revolutionary War.[22]

Washington's opportunities in what became the crisis leading to the American Revolution owed something to his visibility outside Virginia. He was known to have traveled widely in America and to have made at least casual acquaintances from Massachusetts to North Carolina. He was warmly received in New York City when he took his stepson Jackie there to enroll at King's College. Jackie's status, because of his wealth and Washington connection, is suggested by the fact that he was allegedly the only student at the school to take his meals with the faculty. Few of the

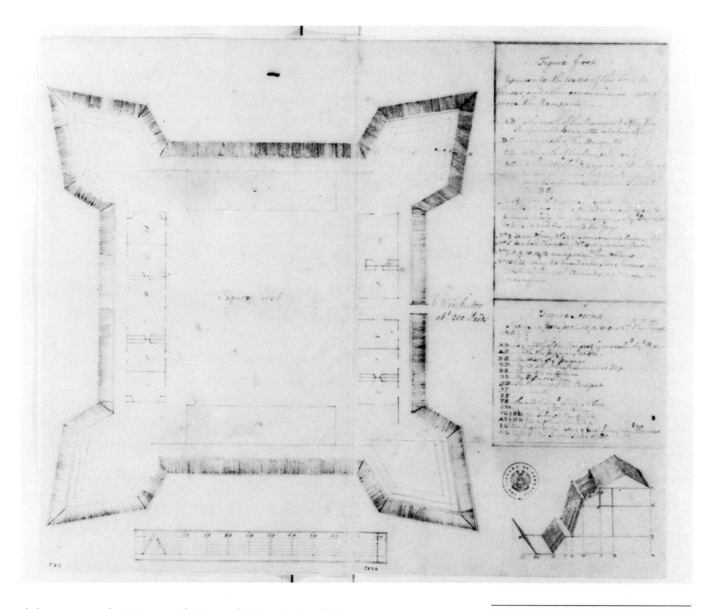

delegates to the First and Second Continental Congresses were as well-traveled as Washington. Even John and Samuel Adams, celebrated for their part in the resistance movement against British threats to American liberties, had seemingly never been outside the colony of Massachusetts. Washington, on a wider horizon, was known to have made history. He had published an account of his part in events that led to the French and Indian War, the American phase of the European Seven Years' War. In London, he had appeared for the first time in works of history, John Entick's *A New Naval History* and William Livingston's *A Review of the Military Operations in North America.*[23]

When Virginia's legislators, meeting in extralegal conventions, put Washington near the head of their list of representatives to the intercolonial gatherings in Philadelphia in 1774–1775, they did not do so because of Washington's standing as a legislative chieftain or a noted parliamentarian. Nor was he out in front of such fiery opponents of British imperial aggression as Richard Henry Lee,

"Plan of Fort Loudoun," *c.*1756–1758. After Braddock's Defeat in 1755, Colonel George Washington established his headquarters in Fredericktown, Virginia (later Winchester). He constructed Fort Loudoun, named for the new commander of British forces in America, as one of a chain of western Virginia forts built to protect settlers from French and Indian raids. *(Library of Congress, Washington, D.C.)*

Patrick Henry, and Thomas Jefferson, but he was rapidly becoming their equal in his determination to uphold American liberties by every possible means. He was chosen because of his intercolonial visibility and because of his well-known military record at a time when an armed response to Britain was becoming more than a remote possibility.

NOTES

1. Paul K. Longmore, *The Invention of George Washington* (Berkeley and Los Angeles, 1988), 145–58.

2. "Sentiments on a Peace Establishment," [1783], in John C. Fitzpatrick, ed., *The Writings of George Washington*, Vol. 26, *January–December 1783* (Washington, D. C., 1938), 389.

3. Washington to John Augustine Washington, 28 May 1755, in W. W. Abbot, ed., *The Papers of George Washington, Colonial Series*, Vol. 1, *1748–August 1755* (Charlottesville, Va., 1983), 289–90.

4. Robert Dinwiddie to Washington, June 27, 1754, Washington to Dinwiddie, August 21, 1754, in Abbot, ed., *Papers of George Washington, Colonial Series*, Vol. 1, *1748–August 1755* (Charlottesville, Va., 1983), 50, 192–93; H. R. McIlwaine et al., eds., *Executive Journals of the Council of Colonial Virginia*, Vol. 5 (Richmond, 1925–1966), 412–13.

5. This episode marks an early phase of Washington's lifetime interest in the North American interior. The subject is treated comprehensively in a collection of essays edited by Warren R. Hofstra, *George Washington and the Virginia Backcountry* (Madison, Wis., 1998).

6. Washington to John Augustine Washington, 31 May 1754, in Abbot, ed., *The Papers of George Washington, Colonial Series*, Vol. 1, *1748–August 1755* (Charlottesville, Va., 1983), 118.

7. Washington to William Fitzhugh, 15 November 1754, in ibid., 225–26.

8. Washington to John Robinson, 20 April 1755, in ibid., 256, 255.

9. Robert Orme to Washington, 2 March 1755, Washington to Robert Orme, 15 March 1755, Washington to John Augustine Washington, 14 May 1755 in ibid., 241, 242–45, 278.

10. Washington to Mary Ball Washington, 18 July 1755, in ibid., 336.

11. Washington to Mary Ball Washington, 18 July 1755, Washington to Robert Dinwiddie, 18 July 1755, in ibid., 336, 339.

12. Don Higginbotham, *George Washington and the American Military Tradition* (Athens, Ga., 1985), 9, 140; Joseph Ball to Washington, 5 September 1755, in Abbot, ed., *The Papers of George Washington, Colonial Series*, Vol. 2, *August 1755–April 1756* (Charlottesville, Va., 1983), 15–16.

13. James Titus, *The Old Dominion at War: Society, Politics, and Warfare in Late Colonial Virginia* (Columbia, S.C., 1991).

14. Higginbotham, *George Washington*, chap. 1.

15. "Instructions to Company Commanders," 29 July 1757, in Abbot, ed., *The Papers of George Washington, Colonial Series*, Vol. 4, *November 1756–October 1757* (Charlottesville, Va., 1984), 344.

16. "Memorial to John Campbell, Earl of Loudoun," 23 March 1757, in ibid., 112–14.

17. William H. Browne, ed., *Correspondence of Governor Horatio Sharpe* (Baltimore, 1888–1895), 1: 416.

18. Washington to Mary Ball Washington, 30 September 1757, in Abbot, ed., *The Papers of George Washington, Colonial Series*, Vol. 4, *November 1756–October 1757* (Charlottesville, Va., 1984), 430; "List of Deaths for the Year 1757," *The Gentlemen's Magazine* 27 (1757): 531.

19. For correspondence concerning William Henry Fairfax, see Abbot, ed., *The Papers of George Washington, Colonial Series*, Vol. 5, *October 1757–September 1758* (Charlottesville, Va., 1988), 17, 70–71, 136–37.

20. Washington to John Stanwix, 10 April 1758; Washington to Thomas Gage, 12 April 1758, in ibid., 117–18, 126.

21. "Address from the Officers of the Virginia Regiment," 31 December 1758, in Abbot, ed., *The Papers of George Washington, Colonial Series*, Vol. 6, *September 1758–December 1760* (Charlottesville, Va., 1988), 179–81.

22. The full text of the sermon appears in William B. Sprague, ed., *Sermons by the Rev. Samuel Davies* (Philadelphia, 1863), 3: 99–101. Also in *Virginia Gazette* (Purdie), 12 December 1777.

23. John Entick, *A New Naval History: or, Compleat View of the British Marine, in which the Royal Navy and the Merchant's Service are Traced through All Their Periods and Different Branches* . . . (London, 1757), 841–42; *William Livingston, A Review of the Military Operations in North America* (London, 1757), 6–7 and reprinted, 1758, 1770.

Young Washington

AMBITION,

ACCOMPLISHMENT,

AND ACCLAIM

Rosemarie Zagarri
George Mason University

Biography and Autobiography

TWO

WASHINGTON'S "REMARKS"
IN CONTEXT

GEORGE WASHINGTON never wrote the story of his life. Partly to avoid any imputation of vanity, he decided early on to leave that business to others. The closest he came was the autobiographical "Remarks," a short essay that covers only a small fraction of his eventful life. Washington, however, did not intend for the "Remarks" to survive. He wrote the comments at the specific request of his friend and former aide-de-camp, Lieutenant Colonel David Humphreys. Working with Washington's full cooperation and agreement, Humphreys prepared what we would call an "authorized" biography of Washington's life, dealing with the period from his birth to his retirement after the American Revolution. After writing a draft, Humphreys asked his subject to read what he had written. Washington then commented on the manuscript, producing notes keyed to specific pages in the text.

Washington's observations—the "Remarks"—were meant to explain, correct, or clarify particular points in Humphreys' work. Modestly apologizing for "the badness of his memory," he hoped that his friend might find something of use. "If there are any grains among them," he said, "Colo. H. can easily separate them from the chaff." He was quite insistent, however, about the disposition of the manuscript. "It is earnestly requested that after Colo. Humphreys has extracted what he shall judge necessary, and given it in his own language, that the *whole* of what Is here contained may be returned to G.W., or committed to the flames."[1]

Much to our benefit, Humphreys ignored the General's wishes. As Washington hoped, Humphreys did separate the wheat from the chaff. Although he never published a full-length biography, he did incorporate Washington's changes into a biographical sketch that was published several times between 1789 and 1794. Instead of destroying or returning the document, however, Humphreys kept the "Remarks" in his possession. After his death in 1818, the work passed to his wife, who subsequently presented it to John Pickering, the son of a close family friend. After many years in the Pickering family, the document was purchased in 1974 by John Fleming, a respected dealer and collector, and then sold as part of the Fleming estate at auction in 1988 to Malcolm Forbes. The Allegheny Conference on Community Development, on behalf of the French and Indian War sites in western Pennsylvania, purchased the work in 2002, bringing the manuscript to a new, and more appropriate, home in Pittsburgh, near the site of many of the events described in the manuscript.[2] The best way to understand the "Remarks," then, is as part of Humphreys' larger project.

Long before Humphreys became Washington's biographer, he was the General's military aide. Born in Derby, Connecticut in 1752, Humphreys graduated from Yale and took a job as a schoolmaster. The coming of the American Revolution opened up a whole new range of opportunities for the ambitious young man. Volunteering in 1776 as an adjutant with the Second Connecticut Militia Regiment, he quickly made his way up the military hierarchy, becoming a brigade major at age twenty-five and a lieutenant colonel at twenty-eight. Even more significant were the positions of trust he occupied. Only two years after enlisting, he became an aide-de-camp to General Israel Putnam, one of Washington's four major generals. In May 1780, he was appointed aide to General Nathanael Greene; shortly thereafter, he was transferred to Washington's military family.[3]

Significantly, Humphreys' appointments seem to have had as much to do with his literary acumen as his military prowess. During lulls in the fighting, Humphreys had begun to express his patriot sentiments in verse. In the winter of 1779–80, he wrote a

Colonel David Humphreys (1752–1818, B.A. 1771, M.A. 1774, Yale University) c.1807–1808, by Gilbert Stuart. George Washington wrote the autobiographical "Remarks," responding to a draft biography by his friend and aide David Humphreys. Colonel Humphreys, a loyal member of Washington's staff during the Revolution and later secretary to the president, never completed the biography but published parts of it anonymously. *(Yale University Art Gallery, Gift of Mrs. David Humphreys)*

poem called "An Address to the Armies" that praised American soldiers and celebrated their military leaders. Even before it was published, Humphreys sent a copy to General Greene, who soon requested the poet's reassignment to his command. Not long after joining Greene's staff, Humphreys received the printed version, which he forwarded to General Washington. In one of several similar passages, Humphreys described Washington's leadership in these terms:

> *When lo! to guide us through the storm of war,*
> *Beam'd the bright splendor of Virginia's star.*
> *His voice inspir'd, his godlike presence led.*
> *The Britons saw, and from his presence fled.*[4]

Shortly thereafter he received his new position. Over the years, Washington and Humphreys developed a close personal relationship. Although Washington had strong connections with many of his military aides, Humphreys appears to have been one of his favorites. He was known, according to the poet John Trumbull, as the "belov'd of Washington."[5]

A letter written several years later suggests that Washington was not unaware of the benefits of having his own Boswell at his side. Writing to the Marquis de Lafayette in 1788, Washington recommended the author Joel Barlow to the care of his French comrade. Barlow, according to Washington, was considered "to be one those Bards who hold the keys of the gate by which Patriots, Sages and Heroes are admitted to immortality. Such are your Antient Bards who are both the priest and door-keepers to the temple of fame." Lest the Marquis disparage such a thought, Washington added, these "are no vulgar functions. Men of real talents in Arms have commonly approved themselves patrons of the liberal arts and friends to the poets of their own as well as former times. In some instances by acting reciprocally, heroes have made poets, and poets heroes."[6] True to this formula, Washington would make Humphreys his poet and Humphreys would make Washington his hero.

After the Revolution ended, Washington famously resigned his commission and returned to private life at Mount Vernon. With Washington's help, Humphreys secured a diplomatic position negotiating commercial treaties for the United States in Europe. As early as 1784, Humphreys wrote to Washington suggesting the need for a biography of the General that would, he said, place "your actions in the true point of light in which pos-

terity ought to view them."[7] Subtly and then overtly, Humphreys put himself forward for the task, proposing to write a full account that drew on his mentor's papers and correspondence. After some initial hesitation, Washington consented. Praising Humphreys' suitability for the job, he commented, "I should be pleased indeed to see you undertake this business; your abilities as a writer; your discernment respecting the principles which lead to the decision by arms; your personal knowledge of many facts . . . & your diligence in investigating truth . . . fit you . . . for this task."[8] To facilitate the endeavor, he issued Humphreys, who was unmarried at the time, a standing invitation to reside with Washington and his family at Mount Vernon.

Arriving from Europe in 1786, Humphreys visited Washington for six weeks and began to set to work on the biography. Political ambition and personal concerns drew him back to his home state of Connecticut for a time. During this time, he coauthored with the "Connecticut Wits" a biting satire called "The Anarchiad: A

"View of Mount Vernon looking towards the Southwest," 1796, by Benjamin Henry Latrobe. English immigrant architect and artist Latrobe (1764–1820) visited the Washington family home at the end of the President's second term. He recorded the spectacular Potomac River view from the front porch of the Mount Vernon mansion. (*Maryland Historical Society, Baltimore, Maryland*)

Poem on the Restoration of Chaos and Substantial Night," on the weaknesses of government under the Articles of Confederation.[9] Then in November 1787, Humphreys returned to Mount Vernon, where he stayed until Washington left to assume the presidency in April 1789. Prior to Humphreys' arrival, Washington made only one demand of his young protégé: "in all things you shall do as you as you please."[10] Humphreys appears to have abided by the General's wishes. During this time, he served as Washington's dinner companion, sounding board, adviser, and friend, part of an inner circle that included only eight people—Washington's wife, his two grandchildren, his nephew and his wife, his secretary Tobias Lear, and Humphreys. During this time, Humphreys wrote poems, translated a French play into English, and produced an essay on the life of another of his mentors, General Israel Putnam.[11]

Humphreys also worked on the Washington biography. Focusing on the period from Washington's birth to his retirement after the revolutionary war, he produced a manuscript that looked back to the General's past achievements, especially during the French and Indian War, rather than anticipated his future political career.[12] Significantly, too, Humphreys was more interested in presenting Washington's early life and his present-day activities rather than in recounting his exploits during the American Revolution. "It is the less necessary to particularize, his transactions in the course of the late war," he said, "because the impression which he made is yet fresh in every mind."[13] At some point after Washington's election, probably in early 1789, Humphreys did compose additional sections relating to Washington's acceptance of the presidency, but these parts remained sketchy and unfinished. They were not part of the document Washington read when he produced his "Remarks."[14]

Humphreys' unique access to Washington represented both a strength and a weakness of the work. His account tended to portray Washington in a most favorable light, emphasizing his exemplary character, military leadership, and high sense of personal morality and discipline. Stating his purpose, Humphreys asserted, "Should the success [of the biography] be in proportion to the subject—future Generations will rejoice in finding in one point of view so many facts relative to a man, who received, while living, the unlimited applause of his Countrymen; to his memory, when dead, the incense of gratitude will not cease to be offered; and whose examples of private morality will forever be cited by parents for the imitation of their sons—: Nor need we fear to predict, that, so long as the imperial fabric which he has assisted to raise shall endure, heroes will be proud to emulate his military virtues, senates continue to inculcate the practice of his political precepts, and infants be taught to lisp the name of their country's benefactor in their first efforts of articulation."[15]

Given this purpose, and his expectation that Washington would read what he wrote, it is not surprising that Humphreys glossed over or failed to mention sensitive matters, such as Washington's failed attempts to secure a British commission during the Seven Years' War, his penchant for land speculation, or his ownership of black slaves. He delicately referred to Washington's chronic bowel problem, what Washington himself called "an inveterate disorder in his Bowels," as a "pulmonary complaint."[16] The closest he came to criticizing his mentor was to repeat a statement made by Washington's subordinates during the American Revolution: that the commander in chief "sometimes exposed his own person too much, especially in reconnoitring the enemy. In some instances, it would not have been difficult to have killed or taken him prisoner."[17] Such a criticism was, of course, also a testament to Washington's bravery.

Nonetheless, Humphreys' closeness to Washington enabled him to write an account that few others could. In the draft manuscript, Humphreys emphasized the importance of his personal relationship with his subject. "To the Writer of these memoirs on General Washington, a consciousness of possessing an uncommon share in his confidence &, in many instances, a full knowledge of his motives, together with a promise from him of whatever manuscript or oral communications were necessary, might have been no inconsiderable inducements to have hazarded the undertaking. But the General's opinion, that the writer was more competent in several respects to the execution of the task than any other, could not fail of being decisive with the latter."[18] Washington, in other words, trusted Humphreys more than any other author to be the chronicler of his life. Although Humphreys was prone to self-promotion, Humphreys proved to be a good choice.

Humphreys' personal connection gave him knowledge of aspects of the General's life that were not widely known. He could speak with authority, for example, about Washington's early education under a private tutor, his mother's resistance to Washington's plan at age fifteen to join the British navy, and his impressive physical strength. "I have several times heard him say," Humphreys noted, that "he never met any man who could throw a stone to so great a distance as himself; and, that when standing in the valley beneath the natural bridge in Virginia, he has thrown one up to that stupendous arch."[19] While we cannot credit Mason L. (Parson) Weems' claim that Washington tossed a silver dollar across the Rappahannock River, we can have some confidence in Humphreys' assertion that Washington could throw a stone that would hit the Natural Bridge. Discussing the American Revolution, Humphreys commented on what he claimed no other writer had thus far noticed. "One of the most amiable & useful services [Washington] rendered to the U.S.," according to Humphreys, was "the wise care he bestowed on & wonderful agency he had in, eradicating the prejudices against each, which existed in an eminent degree between the Inhabitants of the various American Colonies before the Revolution."[20] By facilitating cooperation and diminishing animosity among people from various states, Washington achieved a unity that made victory over the British possible.

Humpheys offered telling details about Washington's life in retirement. From his own personal observation, he could discuss Washington's daily routine at Mount Vernon, his fondness for foxhunting and Madeira wine, and his abiding interest in agricultural experiments and innovations. "Agriculture," according to Humphreys, "is the favorite employment of General Washington, in which he wishes to pass the remainder of his days."[21] Humphreys also offered insights into Washington's personality and temperament. "Notwithstanding his temper is rather of a serious cast & his countenenace commonly carries the impression of thoughtfulness; he perfectly relishes a pleasant story, an unaffected sally of wit, or a burlesque description which surprises by its suddenness & incongruity."[22]

Perhaps most significantly, Humphreys' personal connection gave him something no other biographer has had, before or since: the opportunity to ask Washington to read the work and make his own corrections, additions, and emendations. Once Humphreys had written as much has he could, he gave the original manuscript (which is currently held by the Rosenbach Museum and Library and by Yale University's Sterling Library) to Washington with a request for comments. Washington responded with ten and one-half pages of "Remarks" in his own handwriting. The largest portion of the document—nine pages—concerns Washington's experiences in the Seven Years War. Subsequently Humphreys incorporated many of Washington's comments into the published version of the work. Washington's "Remarks," then are of interest both for the ways in which they modified

Humphreys' account as well as for what they reveal about Washington himself. His comments not only increase the historical accuracy of Humphreys' biographical sketch, but provide a unique perspective on Washington's own sense of self.

To some extent, Washington's remarks simply represent an effort to help Humphreys get the story right. For example, in a blank space in a sentence concerning the agricultural output of Mount Vernon, Washington inserted the remark, "I believe about 7,000 Bushels of wheat and 10,000 bushels of Indian corn was more the staple of the farm."[23] Washington corrected factual statements concerning his early career. He made certain that Humphreys gave his proper age at various points, noting that he was appointed Major before he was twenty years old and indicating that he was "more than 21 years," when he first set out for Fort Duquesne.[24] He emphasized that it was the wish of his eldest half-brother, rather than that of his father, that he "should be bred for an Officer in the British navy." "My father," he poignantly commented, "died when I was only 10 years old."[25] Washington also corrected a statement about his half-brother's military career, noting that Lawrence was appointed adjutant general of Virginia after, not before, a trip to Cartagena.[26]

Other comments, while also factual in nature, were more revealing. The "Remarks" are the closest Washington came to writing his own autobiography. His comments highlight the aspects of his life that Washington felt should be emphasized. As such, they represent the image that Washington wanted to convey to the public, the portrait that he believed suitable for popular consumption. Washington, for example, took obvious pride in his relationship with Native Americans. He provided an interesting sidelight to Humphreys' discussion of his 1753 trip to the Ohio country. It was on this occasion, he said, that a number of Indian tribes with whom he negotiated treaties assigned him the name, "Caunotaucarius," which in English meant, "the Town taker." This name, Washington continued, "being registered in their Manner & communicated to other Nations of Indians, has been remembered by them ever since in all their transactions with him during the late [Revolutionary] war."[27] He also took great satisfaction in his favorite leisure activity, hunting. Although Humphreys mentioned that Washington "keeps a pack of hounds & and in the season indulges himself with hunting once in a week," Washington felt compelled to add, "tho sometimes he goes oftener."[28]

Other comments reveal other, less well-known sides of Washington's personality. There were flashes of envy or resentment.

Biography and Autobiography

WASHINGTON'S
"REMARKS" IN
CONTEXT

Lawrence Washington, *c.*1740, unattributed. Lawrence Washington (1718–1752) was a highly successful planter who married into the aristocratic Fairfax family. He was a vital influence on younger half-brother George who inherited his Mount Vernon Plantation and had an interest in a military career. *(Courtesy of the Mount Vernon Ladies' Association)*

Washington, for example, seemed aggrieved at the size of his inheritance. Humphreys stated that Washington had come into "a large landed property" as his "patrimonial provision."[29] Washington, however, insisted on amending this assertion, pointing out that his father's second son, Augustine, had had many children who had received "a very large portion" of the estate—"perhaps," Washington emphasized, "the best part."[30] This allotment apparently still rankled. He also wanted the full scope of his dedication to his country known. Referring to his role as commander in chief during the Revolution, Washington remarked, "Whether it be necessary to mention that my time & Services were given to the public without compensation, and that every direct and indirect attempt afterwards, to reward them [was refused] . . . you can best judge."[31] Washington, however, clearly thought it was worth mentioning. He wanted credit for his sacrifices.

The "Remarks" also allowed Washington to voice a hostility to Britain that went back to the Seven Years War. Criticizing British policy, he noted that the surprise engagement with Braddock's troops in 1755 had vindicated him. "The folly & consequence of opposing compact bodies to the sparse manner of Indian fighting in woods, which had in a manner been predicted," he said, "was now so clearly verified that from hence forward another mode obtained in all future operations."[32] Recounting a fruitless trip to Williamsburg in 1755 to request additional aid for his troops, he summarized the consequences of Britain's failure to supply sufficient assistance. "As George Washington foresaw, so it happened, the frontiers were continually harrassed—but not having force enough to carry the War to the gates of Du Quesne, he could do no more than distribute the Troops along the Frontiers in Stockaded Forts."[33] A tinge of self-righteousness permeates Washington's comments. Blinded by their own arrogance, British officials had ignored or dismissed his advice at their own peril.

The final insult occurred when the British concocted a plan that would make officers of any rank holding a commission from the Crown superior to all officers holding colonial appointments. In other words, Washington, a colonel appointed by the governor of Virginia, would be outranked by a captain who held his commission from the King. Such a scheme, he said, "was too degrading for George Washington to submit to; accordingly, he resigned his Military employment."[34] Subsequently, after Washington and others complained in person to Governor Shirley, the commander of British forces in America, Britain offered "a new arrangement" that was more satisfactory.[35] In his "Remarks,"

William Shirley, 1750, by Thomas Hudson. In spite of limited military experience, Royal Governor of Massachusetts Shirley (1694–1771) became the commander of British forces after the death of General Braddock in 1755. Shirley was soon replaced but not before he was visited in Boston by Colonel George Washington requesting more status and seniority for colonial officers. *(National Portrait Gallery, Smithsonian Institution)*

then, Washington lashed out at those who had underestimated him—and his countrymen—many years before. Although Washington's eventual support for the American Revolution was much more than a grudge match, the seeds of his opposition to Britain were planted long before.

Washington's "Remarks" also provides unique insights into Washington's human side. He appears to be more vulnerable and empathetic than either the mythic figure or the wooden caricature would suggest. Writing about the aftermath of the Braddock massacre, Washington vividly portrays his response to the carnage. "The shocking scenes which presented themselves in this Nights march are not to be described—The dead—the dying—the groans—lamentations—and crys along the Road of the wounded for help . . . were enough to pierce a heart of adamant."[36] This is Washington as an emotional young man experiencing the horrors of war for the first time rather than as a hardened war veteran who led American forces to victory in the American Revolution.

A similar sense of vulnerability appears in another episode, an incident that Washington found so painful that he apparently never mentioned it anywhere else in his papers or correspondence. On November 12, 1758, the British were pressing northward toward Fort Duquesne in a desperate effort to beat the onset of winter. Lookouts sent word that the French were approaching their position at Loyalhanna in southwestern Pennsylvania. According to Washington's account, Lieutenant Colonel Mercer and his troops were sent to deter the enemy. Embroiled in a prolonged exchange of fire, the British appeared to lose ground. At that point, Washington received General Forbes's permission to march to Mercer's aid and provide reinforcements. But it was a dark and foggy day, and dusk was setting in. Speaking in the third person, Washington remembered with horror what happened next.

[Washington] detached Scouts . . . to communicate his approach to his friend Colo[nel] Mercer advancing slowly in the meantime—But it being near dusk and the intelligence not having been fully dissiminated among Colonel Mercers Corps, and they taking us, for the enemy who had retreated approaching in another direction commenced a heavy fire upon the releiving party which drew fire in return in spite of all the exertions of the Officers one of whom & several privates were killed and many wounded before a stop could be put to it. To accomplish which G[eorge] W[ashington] never was in more imminent danger by

George Washington's British silver-mounted small sword, 1757. Seeking the proper trappings of a regular British officer, Colonel Washington ordered this ornate sword from a London merchant in 1756 and probably carried it to Fort Ligonier in 1758. He wore it for his 1772 Peale portrait and at his inauguration as the first U.S. president in 1789. *(Courtesy of the Mount Vernon Ladies' Association)*

being between two fires, knocking up with his sword the presented pieces.[37]

This episode of what we would call "friendly fire" left at least fourteen men dead and many others wounded.[38]

What is most remarkable in the account is that even after thirty years Washington's sense of fear, grief, and personal responsibility are still palpable. The dangers he encountered as commander in chief seemed to pale in comparison with what he felt as a young man responsible for leading his men into mortal danger from other members of His Majesty's troops. He tried to end the debacle by walking between the two lines of fire and knocking muskets up with his sword. This action, he noted, put his life "in as much jeopardy as it had ever been before or since."[39] Only after three decades could Washington bear to write about it—and only then to his trusted friend David Humphreys.

Humphreys himself never finished writing the full-length biography of Washington that he had initially proposed. Until recently, it was believed that he never published the work at all. However, in the course of research on an earlier project I discovered that Humphreys did indeed publish a revised version of the sketch he had shown Washington—but not under his own name. The work first appeared in 1789 as a chapter in Jedidiah Morse's *The American Geography; or, A View of the Present Situation in the United States of America.* Subsequently, the biography was reprinted anonymously as a pamphlet in 1790, 1792, and 1794. It also appeared in the *Massachusetts Magazine* in 1789 and surfaced in further revised forms after Washington's death. The published versions removed all references to Humphreys and to the author's personal relationship with Washington. Although the print versions did incorporate Washington's "Remarks," they did not indicate that Washington had vetted the draft manuscript. Interestingly, Washington's extended discussion of the Seven Years' War was condensed to only four long paragraphs.[40]

But why, after all that effort, did Humphreys dispose of the manuscript in this fashion? The developments of the late 1780s may have led Humphreys to reconsider the wisdom of the larger initial project. For a variety of reasons, it seems that Humphreys abandoned the idea of completing a full-length biography of Washington. Once it became clear that Washington would be reentering public life, he may have sensed that any biography would be incomplete, if not premature. Washington's life would now have many more chapters. In addition, Humphreys no doubt expected his own life to take a new turn, which it did. Humphreys accompanied Washington to New York when he assumed the presidency and served for a time as his personal secretary. Throughout the 1790s he held various diplomatic posts in Portugal and Spain. In 1793 he even undertook a special mission to negotiate for the release of the Algerine captives. Given the press of public duties, Humphreys no longer had the leisure with which to complete a comprehensive biography.[41]

Humphreys also knew that his friend and fellow author, Jedidiah Morse, was completing a geography describing the history, topography, and culture of the young United States. Humphreys had, in fact, written a letter of introduction to Washington for Morse in 1786 when he traveled throughout the United States gathering information for the volume. Morse acknowledged, however, that one individual alone could not could not author the entire geography. "The nature of the work," he said in a letter to another friend, "does not admit of much originality. The book must derive merit—if it have any—from the accuracy and good judgment with which it is *compiled*, rather than the genius with which it is *composed*. To save me from the odious character of Plagarist, general credit will be given in the preface for all sections inserted in the work. To particularize such would be needless and endless."[42] Indeed, in the preface to the *American Geography*, Morse did generally acknowledge others' contributions, saying that he "frequently used the words as well as the ideas of [other] writers, although the reader has not been particularly apprized of it."[43]

Thus it seems reasonable that Humphreys may have offered Morse his short biography of Washington, or given it to him if asked. This solution had several benefits. Humphreys' sketch would provide a fitting complement to Morse's description of the country that Washington had done so much to help found. Humphreys, moreover, would have the satisfaction of knowing that an accurate rendering of Washington's early career was in print. Once Morse's *American Geography* appeared in 1789, other publications quickly drew on it for their accounts of Washington's life. By not claiming authorship, Humphreys would avoid any imputation of conflict of interest that might otherwise arise. He may have suspected that Washington, with his strict sense of propriety, might disapprove of his publishing the work under his own name at a time when he held public office. Anonymity would give the work the appearance of objectivity. Although Humphreys might choose at a later date to return to the project, this format would do for the time being.

Others, though, would write about Washington's life. Soon after Washington's death, Parson Weems published his largely fictitious account. In 1807, Supreme Court Justice John Marshall produced a multi-volume tome. Many other Washington biographies would follow over the years.[44] Yet Humphreys' biographical sketch along with Washington's "Remarks" continue to offer a unique portrait. Taken together, these documents provide a fascinating glimpse into Washington's life at a key moment: after the Revolution but before the presidency. We see a Washington who was a real person—a man sickened by the screams of his wounded troops, touched by the appeals of his subordinates, and piqued by those who crossed him. He liked to hunt foxes, drink wine, and listen to jokes. He was neither an aloof stick-figure nor an earnest do-gooder. Yet his immense bravery, sense of honor, and personal integrity were as apparent in his private life as his public deeds. As Humphreys remarked in 1800 after receiving word of his friend and mentor's death, "[Washington's] reputation as one of the principal persons engaged in founding the American Republic may safely be trusted to the page of history."[45] Whether Washington knew it or not, his "Remarks" would help secure that reputation.

1. George Washington, "Remarks," War for Empire, Inc., Pittsburgh, 13 (hereinafter referred to as "Remarks." The page numbers refer to the facsimile in this volume.) See transcript above, 24.

2. For a more detailed discussion of this and other issues discussed in this essay, see my Introduction to *David Humphreys' "Life of General Washington" with George Washington's "Remarks,"* ed. Rosemarie Zagarri (Athens, Ga., 1991), xiii–li.

3. Edward M. Cifelli, *David Humphreys* (Boston, 1982), 15–19.

4. "Address to the Armies of the United States of America," in *The Miscellaneous Works of David Humphreys* (1804; reprint, ed. William K. Bottorff, Gainesville, Fla., 1968), 9; Leon Howard, *The Connecticut Wits* (Chicago, 1943), 122–23.

5. Quoted in Douglas Southall Freeman, *George Washington: A Biography*, 7 vols. (New York, 1948–1957), vol. 6, insert between 63–64; Emily Stone Whiteley, *Washington and His Aides-de-Camp* (New York, 1936), 188–207.

6. GW to the Marquis de Lafayette, May 28, 1788 in John C. Fitzpatrick, ed., *The Writings of George Washington from the Original Manuscript Sources, 1745–1799*, 39 vols. (Washington, D.C., 1931–1944). Special thanks to Dr. Pete Henriques for bringing this letter to my attention.

7. Frank Landon Humphreys, *The Life and Times of David Humphreys*, 2 vols. (1917; reprint, St. Clair Shores, Mich., 1971), I: 318.

8. Ibid., I: 330.

9. The other "Connecticut Wits" were John Trumbull, Timothy Dwight, and Joel Barlow. Howard, *Connecticut Wits*, 180–81.

10. Humphreys, *Life and Times*, I: 424–26.

11. Ibid., I: 428–29; Cifelli, *David Humphreys*, 74–76; Howard, *Connecticut Wits*, 246–47.

12. The manuscript version of Humphreys' biography is located in two respositories, scattered throughout Humphreys' other notes and writings. It is in unfinished form. David Humphreys, "The Life of General Washington," 2 vols. AMS 1079/6, Rosenbach Museum and Library, Philadelphia; "The Life of General Washington," Humphreys-Marvin-Olmsted Collection, Box 4, Folder 151, Yale University Sterling Library, Manuscript and Archives Division. I have reconstructed the biography in *David Humphreys' "Life of Washington,"* 3–57.

13. Zagarri, ed., *David Humphreys' "Life of Washington,"* 30.

14. In a section written at a later date (and probably not seen by Washington), Humphreys even provided a glimpse of Washington's agonizing struggle over whether or not he should accept the presidency of the United States. Although most people at the time assumed his acquiescence, Washington himself had serious reservations. Humphreys claimed to be the first person Washington spoke to about the

subject, expressing reluctance to leave his life at Mount Vernon, fearing that he would be charged with hypocrisy for coming out of retirement and doubtful that he was the man best-suited for the job. In a conversation lasting four hours, Humphreys claimed to have persuaded him to postpone his ultimate decision. In the ensuing months, Humphreys and others finally convinced him to accept the office, but he did so, according to Humphreys, with the utmost reluctance. When formal word of his election arrived, Washington reportedly said, "I think I feel very much like a man who is condemned to death does when the time of his execution draws nigh." See Zagarri, ed., *David Humphreys' "Life of Washington,"* xxii, xlv–xlix, 44–51, 54. Quote on 50.

15. Ibid., 5.

16. "Remarks," 11. See transcript above, 23. Zagarri, ed., *David Humphreys' "Life of Washington,"* 24.

17. This was in a section Humphreys wrote after Washington's death. Zagarri, ed., *David Humphreys' "Life of Washington,"* 57.

18. Ibid., 4.

19. Ibid., 6–8.

20. Ibid., 32.

21. Ibid., 36–37.

22. Ibid., 36.

23. Ibid., 24; "Remarks," 13. See transcript above, 24.

24. Zagarri, ed., *David Humphreys' Life of Washington,"* 8–9; "Remarks," 3. See transcript above, 15. For a more detailed discussion of Washington's early career, see Don Higginbotham's essay in chapter 1.

25. "Remarks," 3. See transcript above, 15.

26. Zagarri, ed., *David Humphreys' "Life of Washington,"* 8; "Remarks," 3. See transcript above, 15.

27. "Remarks," 3. See transcript above, 16. For a fuller discussion of the significance of Washington's Indian name, see Fred Anderson's essay in chapter 3, note 21.

28. Zagarri, ed., *David Humphreys' "Life of Washington,"* 37; "Remarks," 13. See transcript above, 24.

29. Zagarri, ed., David Humphreys' "Life of Washington," 6, 8.

30. "Remarks," 3. See transcript above, 15.

31. Ibid., 13. See transcript above, 24.

32. Ibid., 9. See transcript above, 21.

33. Ibid., 10. See transcript above, 22.

34. Ibid., 6. See transcript above, 18.

35. Ibid., 10. See transcript above, 22.

36. Ibid., 9. See transcript above, 20.

37. Ibid., 11. See transcript above, 23.

38. For a contemporary account of the incident, see W. W. Abbot, ed., *The Papers of George Washington, Colonial Series,* Vol. 6, *September 1758–December 1760* (Charlottesville, 1988), 121–23, n.5. For historians' accounts, see Freeman, *George Washington,* 2: 357–58; James Thomas

Flexner, *George Washington: The Forge of Experience (1732–1775)* (Boston, 1965), 216–17.

39. "Remarks," 10. See transcript above, 23.

40. Zagarri, ed., David Humphreys' "Life of Washington," xxvii–xxxi; Jedidiah Morse, *The American Geography; or, A View of the Present Situation of the United States of America* (Elizabethtown, N.J., 1789), 127–32; *A True and Authentic History of His Excellency George Washington, Commander in Chief of the American Army during the late War, and present President of the United States* (Philadelphia, 1790), 2–10; *The Life of General Washington, Commander in Chief of the American Army during the Late War, and present President of the United States* (Philadelphia, 1794), 4–22; Elhanan Winchester, *Oration* (London, 1792); *The Massachusetts Monthly Magazine; or Monthly Museum* (May 1789), 286–90. For other examples, see William S. Baker, *Early Sketches of George Washington reprinted with Bibliography and Bibliographical Notes* (Philadelphia, 1904), 124–25.

41. Cifelli, *David Humphreys*, 95–96, 101–02, 118–20.

42. Quoted in William B. Sprague, *The Life of Jedidiah Morse, D.D.* (New York, 1874), 196.

43. Morse, *American Geography*, vi.

44. For excerpts from various biographies of Washington, see Morton Borden, ed., *George Washington: Great Lives Observed* (Englewood Cliffs, N.J., 1969), 108–46.

45. Zagarri, ed., *David Humphreys' "Life of Washington,"* 57.

Fred Anderson
University of Colorado, Boulder

"Just As They Occurred To The Memory, They Were Committed"

Three

SPECULATIONS ON GEORGE WASHINGTON'S AUTOBIOGRAPHICAL "REMARKS" OF 1787

ESPITE the lack of formal education that made him self-conscious about his writing, George Washington wrote a great deal during his life—fully as much as any other important leader of the Revolution, and more than enough to fill ninety volumes in the definitive edition of his writings that is now more than halfway to completion.[1] Writing was a habit that Washington formed early and nurtured long. He started his first diary on 11 March 1748, when at the age of sixteen he assisted in surveying lands in the Shenandoah Valley; he made his last entry with an observation of the temperature ("Mer[cury] 28") on the night of 13 December 1799, twenty-four hours before he died.[2] Over the intervening half-century, he produced tens of thousands of letters, memoranda, orders, addresses, and other documents, taking great care that copies of the most important papers should be preserved. Late in life he undertook the Herculean task of correcting and arranging them. In the summer of 1798, he reported, he was giving "all [his] leisure hours" to "the arrangement, and overhaul of my voluminous Public Papers—Civil and Military—that, they may go into secure deposits—and, hereafter, into hands that may be able to separate the grain from the chaff."[3]

Washington, then, anticipated that future Americans would take a keen interest in his life and also that they would find much that was unremarkable in his papers. This was because he understood that most of what he had written had been for practical and immediate purposes. His diaries tracked information, events, and conditions useful to him as surveyor, soldier, land speculator, and planter. Hence, for example, his assiduous attention to recording weather conditions: such diary entries strike modern readers as inconsequential, but they were of great importance to a man whose income depended on raising crops and livestock for market. He maintained a series of letterbooks for similarly practical reasons. He needed copies of his business correspondence because he could not operate his plantations efficiently and economically without an accurate, accessible record of bargains struck, lands bought, loans contracted, debts paid, slaves sold, merchandise ordered, and so on.

All such practical and private writings, Washington assumed, would be "chaff" to future readers. He spent the time and energy he did in ordering his "public"—that is military and political—correspondence because he quite reasonably anticipated that historians would ransack it for evidence concerning the Revolution. As early as the mid-1780s he was beginning to edit his writings from the 1750s, crossing out and rewriting passages in his oldest letterbooks in order to clarify what he saw, in retrospect, as his original intent. The only possible reason for editing these letters as he did was that he expected latter-day historians and biographers, seeking to explain his career as the commander in chief of the Continental Army, to scrutinize his early military experience for the roots of later achievements. His "corrections" suggest that he wanted them to find a more polished and mature man than the young Colonel Washington had, in fact, been.[4]

Given his tirelessness as a writer and his evident determination to leave a record of his life that depicted his actions and behavior in terms consistent with his own understanding of them, it may seem surprising that Washington never attempted to

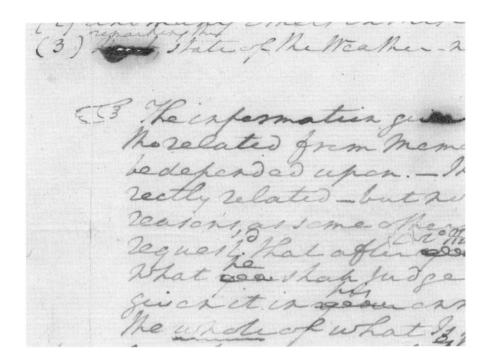

write an autobiography. His willingness to let others tell the story of his life distinguishes him from other elder statesmen of the Revolution: John Adams, Benjamin Franklin, and Thomas Jefferson all composed memoirs in which they imposed plots of their own devising on their lives and times. We cannot, in the end, know the reasons for Washington's reticence. It may offer evidence of a humility deeper than any that Adams, Franklin, or Jefferson could claim, or bespeak Washington's lack of confidence in his literary skill; it may simply reflect the demands of an active life that allowed little time for extended reflection. In any case, the fact remains that in all the millions of words he wrote, only a few over 4,000 were given to self-conscious reminiscence: the ten-and-a-half pages of closely-written prose, reproduced in this volume, that he simply called his "Remarks."

Had Washington's own wishes been followed, even those few sheets would not have survived. Conscious that what he had written was "hastily and incorrectly related—but not so much for these reasons, as [for] some others" that he chose not to specify, Washington appended a note to his account which "earnest[ly] request[e]d that . . . the *whole* of what Is here contained may be returned to G.W., or committed to the flames."[5] To make this unmistakably clear, Washington even tried to draw the old printer's symbol of a hand pointing its index finger to his instructions. Fortunately for us, the recipient disregarded his directions. As a result we have what is in every sense a singular document to examine for what it can reveal of how, in the anxious days between the writing and ratification of the Constitution, George

Detail from George Washington's "Remarks," c.1787–1788. Using a tiny pointing hand, an old printer's device to highlight important passages, George Washington stressed a paragraph at the close of his "Remarks." He wanted the document returned "or committed to the flames," a request his aide Colonel Humphreys never honored. (*War for Empire, Inc., Pittsburgh, Pennsylvania*)

Washington remembered the beginnings of his extraordinary career.

That Washington wrote anything at all had less to do with the urgent desire to tell his own tale than with the affection he felt for the man who asked him for his reminiscences—Colonel David Humphreys, who had served as his aide-de-camp during the Revolutionary War. As Rosemarie Zagarri reveals in chapter 2, it also had a great deal to do with the former aide's persistence. Humphreys first suggested that someone should write Washington's biography in September 1784, hinting that he might be a suitable candidate for the job. Washington failed to take the hint, so Humphreys nominated himself as biographer early in the following year. When Washington still made no response, Humphreys renominated himself several months later. The general finally gave way in mid-1785 with generosity and good grace, inviting Humphreys to be his houseguest while he worked on the project. Humphreys gladly accepted the invitation and spent six weeks at Mount Vernon in the summer of 1786.[6]

The result was the biographical sketch that occasioned Washington's "Remarks." He evidently gave the general a draft version to comment on and correct not long after he returned for a second, and much longer, stay at Mount Vernon, which lasted from November 1787 through Washington's departure to take up the Presidency in March 1789. Because the document bears no date, we do not know precisely when during this period Washington composed the "Remarks." On the basis of internal evidence and certain changes that Humphreys made to his manuscript, however, the editors of *The Papers of George Washington* have placed the document at the end of his writings from December, 1787.[7] If this is an accurate surmise—and there is every reason to think it is—we can establish the temporal context in which Washington wrote. That context allows us to begin making inferences about why he wrote what he did, and what the "Remarks" may have meant to him at the time.

Seventeen eighty-seven had been the worst in the series of bad years that followed Washington's return home from the Continental Army. It was, of course, true that his remarkable leadership in the War of Independence had made him the best-known American citizen then living, while his resignation of command at the end of the war had made him the most revered. Because no revolutionary general had ever voluntarily surrendered power before, Washington was routinely likened to the legendary Cincinnatus, who had been called from his farm to defend Rome

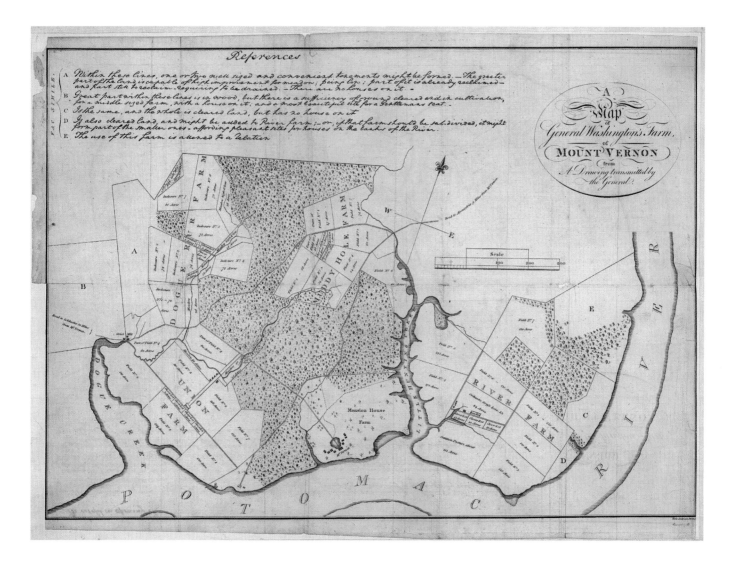

"A Map of George Washington's Farm at Mount Vernon from a Drawing by the General," *c.*1801. In spite of long absences, General Washington, a resourceful farmer, devoted as much time as possible to his plantation's success. He personally surveyed and mapped the several farms and thousands of acres that, with hundreds of slaves, a grist mill and fisheries, made up the large community called Mount Vernon. (*Library of Congress, Washington, D.C.*)

against the invading Aequi, led the army to victory, and then spurned the dictatorship in order to return to the plow.[8] What the admiring world did not understand, however, was just how desperately Washington had wanted to return to his plantations, which by the end of 1783 badly needed his attention.

Washington had been absent from Mount Vernon for nearly nine years. During that time, the estate manager, his mild-mannered cousin Lund Washington, had neglected to collect rents from the local tenants and exercised so little effective control over the slaves that eighteen of them had taken the Revolution's rhetoric literally and freed themselves by running away. Lund never recovered them; worse, he had paid no attention at all to Washington's extensive properties in the Shenandoah and Ohio Valleys. As a result they had been overrun by squatters who refused to pay rent, faked deeds and fraudulently sold his lands, and resisted eviction.[9] When Washington resumed the management of his holdings at the beginning of 1784, he had nearly despaired at the task of restoring order and profitability to his affairs. By late 1787, after four years of trying, the job was far from finished. Taking tenants to court to force the payment of back rents was distasteful and not especially effective as a means of restoring the cash flow he desperately needed. Courts could order tenants to pay, but sheriffs were slow to serve writs of execution, defaulters were apt to flee, and replacement tenants were hard to come by. To make matters worse, little currency circulated in postwar Virginia, and what there was had been badly debased. Even when he was able to collect rents, tenants often paid in commodities—horses, for example—that Washington did not need, and could not sell for a profit.[10]

In 1787 Washington had grown so short of money that he could not pay the taxes due on his land, settle the bill with his doctor, or rent a pew at the parish church.[11] When his mother, claiming she had "Never Lived soe pore," had needed financial help in February, he was able to send her only 15 guineas (£15 15s. sterling). "Which believe me," he wrote in the letter that accompanied the money, "is all I have and which indeed ought to have been paid many days ago to another." He went on to explain his straitened circumstances:

> In the last two years I made no crops. In the first I was obliged to buy Corn and this year have none to sell, and my wheat is so bad I cannot neither eat it myself nor sell it to others, and Tobaca I make none. Those who owe me money cannot or will not pay it without Suits and to sue is like doing nothing, whilst my expences, . . . for the absolute support of my family and the visitors who are constantly here [at Mount Vernon] are exceedingly high; higher indeed than I can support, without selling part of my estate . . . but this I cannot do, without taking much less than the lands I have offered for sale are worth.[12]

Washington had tried hard to revive his fortunes. In the hope of increasing crop yields, he had asked advice from Arthur Young, England's leading expert on scientific agriculture. As a result of Young's generous counsel, he had taken steps to improve the quality of his seed, the design of his plows and other equipment, and his management of the soil. He hoped the new methods might bring relief, but, as he explained to his mother, his crops failed yet again in 1787. Unfortunately for Washington, the benefits of systematic farming lay far in the future.[13]

With similar hopefulness, he had also revived a canal- and road-building project that he had first tried to promote before the Revolution. He imagined that the Potomac, Youghiogheny, and Monongahela rivers could be made into a great highway from the Virginia Tidewater to the Ohio Valley. By easing access to eastern markets, he believed, the tenuous loyalties of the westerners might be secured to the United States rather than the Spanish or the British empires, both of which had agents in the region, intriguing among the Indians and testing the allegiance of white settlers. He also hoped (not coincidentally) that improving communication between the Potomac and the interior would increase the value of the tens of thousands of acres he owned on the Ohio, and on which he had built many plans for future prosperity.[14]

Washington had good reason to worry about the political loyalty of the western settlers. Under the Articles of Confederation, Congress had the authority to sell land from the public domain to settlers, but lacked the resources to take the necessary first steps of buying it from the Indians and surveying it for sale. Congress was, moreover, incapable of imposing American sovereignty on the scores of thousands of hunters, traders, and farmers who had moved west and taken up lands without paying attention to such niceties as legal title. Nor could the United States defend them against the Indians, to whom the British (from forts they still occupied south of the Great Lakes, on American soil) were eagerly selling arms and ammunition. Lacking both the power to impose control on the settlers and the ability to win their loyalty by offering them land and protection, Congress could only watch as events took their course.

This inability to maintain order had become even more urgently manifest in Massachusetts, where a tax revolt by farmers turned violent in the winter of 1786–87. Congress, barely able to muster a quorum, had been incapable of responding when a half-armed mob had threatened to seize the federally-owned cannons, muskets, and ammunition stored in Springfield Arsenal. What was called Daniel Shays's Rebellion seemed to threaten anarchy, and perhaps even social revolution. Without an effective central authority to direct their energies and coordinate their defense, Washington feared, thirteen imperfectly-united states would either fall prey to the anarchic tendencies of their own citizens or succumb to the intrigues of European powers.

Washington had monitored these unsettling developments in Massachusetts by reading newspapers and seeking information from correspondents through the winter and spring. The anxiety he felt for the future of the United States during these months finally convinced him that despite the uncertainty of his own affairs he should join Virginia's delegation to the Constitutional

"Just As They Occurred To The Memory . . ."

Convention in the summer of 1787. Although he contributed almost nothing to the debates, he did what he could to promote a more competent national government by acting as President (moderator) of the Convention and—most of all—by signing his massively prestigious name to the document on 17 September.[15]

He declined to take a public role in Virginia's ratification process because he recoiled from partisan debate, but he was far from indifferent to the outcome. He paid close attention to the early ratification conventions in Delaware, Pennsylvania, and New Jersey, and worried that the Antifederalists would defeat the Constitution when Virginia's convention met in the spring of 1788. All through the fall and winter of 1787 he wrote to influential men in favor of the new plan; one reason, indeed, that he was so happy to have David Humphreys return to Mount Vernon in November was that he needed help with his correspondence. Nevertheless, he remained determined that his position in favor of ratification should not be understood as a public endorsement.[16]

The general had good reasons for wishing his views to remain private. As early as 30 August, when the Constitutional Convention was still in session, rumors circulated in Philadelphia that Washington would "be placed at the head of the new Government."[17] And once the published document revealed that executive authority would reside in a single President, many Americans could not believe that such essentially royal powers as the veto, appointment of officeholders, and commander in chief of the armed forces could be entrusted to anyone except Washington. His reputation for virtue, however—what we would call his political credibility—rested on his willingness to *give up* power, as he had done in resigning his command at the end of the Revolutionary War. If he made his support for the Constitution known, he knew, speculation would grow that he wished to be elected as President.

That disturbed Washington, for several reasons. Most obviously, if he were thought to be seeking the Presidency, opponents of the Constitution might well argue that he had in fact been corrupted by power, and thus that he posed a danger to American liberty. Particularly in closely divided states like Virginia, this suspicion might well be sufficient to defeat the Constitution. Equally important, however, was his own ambivalence about the prospect of being elected. While his sense of honor and obligation had prompted him to accept difficult and dangerous public obligations before, the present disarray in his private affairs was such that the last thing he wanted was another extended absence from Mount Vernon. Moreover, his political principles were both strong and sincere. He knew he could exercise power responsibly, for during the Revolutionary War he had done so in ways no other American ever had. Yet he also retained a healthy republican fear of power, and hence distrusted anyone—himself included—who actively sought it. Finally, he cared deeply about preserving his personal reputation, which he understood as key to his standing in the eyes of History. If he were to become President and fail in the role, he might forfeit the esteem of contemporaries and posterity alike. As a man who dreaded public censure, he was far from eager to run such a risk.[18]

All this, then, formed part of the larger frame around Washington when, late in 1787 or early in 1788, he sat down to correct and comment on David Humphreys' draft version of his life. The result is a curious document indeed. Unlike an essay, an address, or a state paper—all documents that stand on their own and explain themselves to the reader—the "Remarks" responds to David Humphreys' draft, which we may well imagine lay on the desk before Washington as he wrote. The extensive, erudite footnotes that Martin West provides to the transcribed version of the document above clarify the elements of context. Yet even with the notes as a guide, reading the document is still a notably odd experience. Both at the beginning and at the end, the "Remarks" give the disjointed feel one might find in reading the answers to an examination on some obscure topic, which have somehow become separated from the question-sheet: the comments make full sense only in the presence of missing information, the character of which the reader can only guess at. What makes the "Remarks" even more confusing is that Washington seemingly could not decide whether to write about himself in the first person ("My father died when I was only 10 years old") or the third ("Before he was 20 years of age"). In the end the third person for the most part won out, as Washington in effect adopted Humphreys' perspective and referred to himself as "G. W."

At first Washington set out merely to save Humphreys from factual errors. He began with a straightforward, numbered list of corrections, pointing out, for example, that an early plan to send him to sea as a midshipman on a Royal Navy man-of-war had not been the idea of his father (who had died too early to have had much effect on his life) but rather that of his oldest brother, Lawrence, "on whom the general concerns of the family devolved." This resolve held up, however, only through the first

"Just As They Occurred To The Memory . . ."

couple of pages Washington read. As he began to comment on the third page of Humphreys' manuscript, something more interesting began to happen. The passage to which Washington was responding had rather cursorily described his diplomatic mission to the Ohio Country in 1753, noting that "Young Mr Washington" had been sent "to treat with the Savages, and to warn the French to desist from their aggressions," and executed "his Mission with singular industry, intelligence & address."[19] This description obviously failed to capture the experience that the much older Mr. Washington recalled, for his comment emphasized the extraordinary distances and the physical hardships of the journey. He had made the trip, he noted, "in the depth of winter when the face of the Earth was covered with snow and the waters covered with Ice." And it had been no mere jaunt: he had "passed 250 miles thro[ugh] an uninhabited Country . . . to Presque Isle" and back, which meant—to spare Humphreys the trouble of calculation—that "the whole dist[ance] from W[illia]msburgh the then seat of Governm[en]t" and back had been "at least 500 miles."

At this point, it seems, powerful memories were beginning to seize the general. They did not easily let go. Just two sentences further along in Humphreys' text, in response to an attempt to foreshadow the coming "war between the two Kingdoms of England & France, that raged for many years throughout every part of the world,"[20] he broke back in with another comment, unrelated to the passage before him. On his mission to the Ohio, he wrote, as if wishing to add something he had forgotten to mention, the Indians with whom he negotiated—"the half-King (as he was called) and the tribes of Nations" in the Ohio Country—had come to call him "Caunotocarious." With a hint of pride he explained that this was an honorific title that meant "(in English) the Town taker; which name being registered in their Manner & communicated to other Nations of Indians, has been remembered by them ever since." Indians, indeed, had used it in diplomatic and other encounters "with him during the late war"—that is, the War of Independence.[21]

By the time he had finished commenting on page 3 of Humphreys' manuscript, then, Washington was already making connections between his early experiences and the more recent past. What had begun as a kind of fact-checker's consciousness—a mere intention to correct errors and misperceptions—was giving way to the memoirist's desire to see the past not just in recollected fragments, but as a connected set of scenes. It may not be too much to infer that Washington was feeling the tug of a story-line that gave direction, coherence, and significance to his memories.

If this was indeed happening in Washington's mind as he wrote, his next comments become even more significant than they might seem at first glance. Laying aside his pen long enough to read yet another of Humphreys' expository paragraphs (this one explaining how, with the death of the "aged & inactive" Colonel Joshua Fry, command of the Virginia Regiment had passed to young Lieutenant Colonel Washington in the spring of 1754) he picked it up again to respond to the biographer's interjected plea for help:

"Just As They Occurred To The Memory . . ."

> II (NB. here General Washington is requested by David Humphreys to give, in brief, some few of the most interesting facts relative to this & subsequent campaigns . . . untill his own leaving the service; if there should be any thing particularly worthy of preservation; according to the minute scale on which this specimen of biography is intended)[.][22]

What followed in Humphreys' manuscript, evidently, was a sketchy outline of the years from 1754 through 1758, when Washington had led the First Virginia Regiment in the French and Indian War.

With the important exception of Washington's service as General Edward Braddock's aide at the Battle of the Monongahela, Humphreys had found little of compelling interest in Washington's early military adventures.[23] To judge from the nearly 3,800 words that Washington wrote in response, however, the general thought otherwise. The memories that had already begun to cast their spell seem to have possessed him completely as he poured out page after page of reminiscence. Now he was no longer responding to and correcting the incidental details of another man's version of his experiences, but describing purposefully, with a sense of drama and urgency, the factors and events that had shaped his life as a young man at war.

Washington began by apologizing—characteristically, given his self-consciousness about his skills as a writer, but a little disingenuously given the general accuracy of what followed—for the imperfections of his account. Humphreys would find, he warned, that it suffered from "the badness of his memory—loss of [his] Papers—[the] mutilated state, in which those of that date were preserved—and [their] derangement . . . by frequent removals in the late war & want of time to collect and methodize them since."[24] Then, with no longer a pause than it took to write "However, according to the best of his recollection" and to cross out a false start, he launched into a highly coherent narrative, punctuated by series of vividly described scenes.

Washington started with the spring of 1754 as he prepared the Virginia Regiment to march for the Forks of the Ohio, where he intended "to oppose the Incroachment of the French on our Western frontiers." He ended in December 1758, following the French evacuation of Fort Duquesne, when he resigned from Virginia's service, "having seen quiet restored . . . to the Frontiers of his own Country which was the principal inducement to his taking arms."[25] He described the intervening events within a generally chronological framework, but interrupted himself repeatedly with asides, interpolations, circlings-back, analyses, and opinions. The language he used and the patterns of his attention in this long section suggest what preoccupied him as he wrote, unifying his recollections in the form of a story.

Fittingly for a man both trained as a surveyor and determined to communicate the size of the obstacles he had faced, Washington's account of the Virginia Regiment's march to the Ohio Country was quite specific as to distances and conditions. His immediate task was to "open the Roads"—that is, widen what had been footpaths sufficiently to allow the passage of supply wagons and artillery carriages—"almost the whole distance *from Winchester,*" his headquarters in the Shenandoah Valley, "to the Ohio." Winchester, he noted, was "80 miles from Alexandria," the nearest seaport, and hence his ultimate base of supply. The regiment had "just ascended the Lawrel [Laurel] Hill 50 M[iles] short of his object[ive, the Forks of the Ohio]: after a March of 230 Miles from Alexa[ndria,]" when he learned that a powerful French force had already "seized the Post he was pushing to obtain." In a matter of weeks, in other words, notwithstanding the "uncommon difficulties" of "incessant Rains" that "swelled waters of which he had many to cross," he had opened 150 miles of road through the wilderness, only to lose what he had conceived as a race to the Forks. Thus he decided to pull his men "back a few miles, to a place known by the name of the great meadows—abounding in Forage more convenient for the purpose of forming a Magazine," or supply depot, while awaiting the reinforcements that he would need to mount an attack on Fort Duquesne.[26]

A hundred regulars under the command of a Scottish cap-

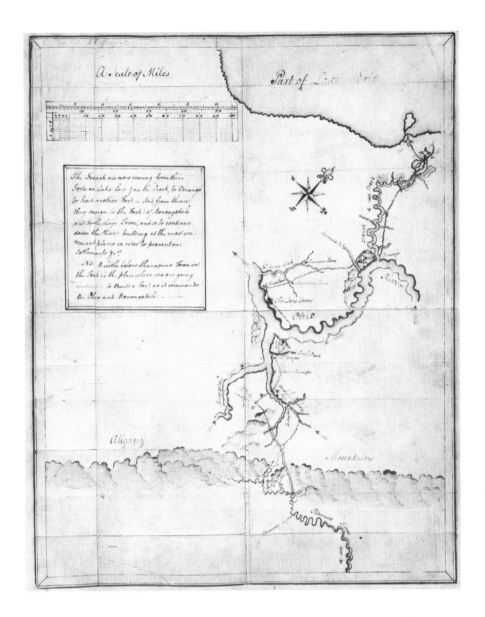

"Map of the river systems from Fort Presque Isle . . . to the Potomac River," 1754, by George Washington. Returning from his famous mission to the French in 1753–1754, 22-year-old surveyor Washington drafted a map of his wilderness route for Virginia and British officials. Hastily prepared from notes and compass readings, the accurate drawing would still be useful today. (*Courtesy of the National Archives, London. Ref. no. MPG 1/118*)

tain—"MacKay a brave & worthy Officer"—did eventually arrive, but Washington never managed to launch the assault he had contemplated.[27] Instead, on 3 July 1754, the French attacked them at the Great Meadows camp he had called Fort Necessity. That they did so was a direct result of an incident Washington barely mentioned in the "Remarks." On 28 May, having learned from the Half-King, Tanaghrisson, that a French detachment had been scouting his position, he "marched at the head of a party, attacked, killed 9 or 10; & captured 20 odd" of the French soldiers.[28] Here Washington's memory lost its specificity in revealing ways. In fact what had happened was that the French commandant at Fort Duquesne had dispatched 35 men under Ensign Joseph Coulon de Villiers de Jumonville to notify Washington that he and his force were unwelcome on ground claimed by the king of France, on whose behalf he was to order them to withdraw. Washington and about 40 of his men, guided by Tanaghrisson's warriors, had sneaked up on the French camp shortly after dawn. The French had looked up from their breakfast to see armed men standing on the rocks above their camp. In the confused firing that broke out immediately thereafter, one Virginian was killed and three were wounded; fourteen Frenchmen were either wounded or killed. The French called for quarter and threw down their arms. As the two groups were attempting to communicate their intentions to each other, Tanaghrisson—apparently hoping to force an unbreakable alliance with the Virginians, and thereby to drive the French from the Forks of the Ohio—split Jumonville's skull with a hatchet. Then he and his men killed all but one of the wounded French prisoners.[29]

At the time Washington had done his best to cover up the massacre, and three decades later still had good reason to represent this, his chaotic baptism of fire, as an event with less significance than in fact it had. But in 1754, Captain Louis Coulon de Villiers, Jumonville's older brother, who led the French and Indian force that attacked Fort Necessity, had entertained no doubts about its significance. He expected to avenge a murder, and on 3 July did just that. It was not, however, part of his plan to start a war between England and France. Thus, after eight hours of unequal combat that left a hundred of Fort Necessity's defenders dead or wounded, Coulon de Villiers ordered a cease-fire and then offered terms of surrender that spared the remains of Washington's battered command. In signing the instrument of capitulation, Washington famously—and unwittingly, for he could not read French—admitted responsibility for the "assassination" of the unfortunate ensign. With that document, Washington had given the French government ample justification for a declaration of war, had they chosen to take it.

As Don Higginbotham points out in chapter 1, Washington had enough supporters in high places that the killing of Jumonville did not immediately destroy his reputation or blight his prospects for military distinction. And by the time he composed the "Remarks," of course, his subsequent career had been distinguished indeed.[30] Thus it is hardly surprising that he would choose not to rehearse this embarrassing, hard-to-explain incident in detail. But that makes it all the more striking that Washington did not similarly elide his description of the defeat he suffered at the hands of Coulon de Villiers on 3 July 1754. Even after the passage of more than three decades, it was as if the twin traumas of battle and defeat remained immediate in his mind, and he still felt the need to account for what had happened.

The battle began, he wrote, when "the Enemy advanced with

Shouts, & dismal Indian yells" in an attempt to overrun the entrenchments that surrounded Fort Necessity's stockade. Finding they could not carry the defenses by storm, the attackers took cover and brought the defenders under musket fire, inflicting heavy casualties. Washington, however, did not choose to describe their tactics in terms so abstract. It was not "from cover" that the enemy fired in his account, but rather "from every little rising—tree—Stump—Stone—and bush [that they] kept up a constant galding [galling] fire upon us." Nor did the Virginians merely suffer "heavy losses" in battle, for "a *full third of our numbers* Officers as well as privates were . . . killed or wounded."[31] Hopelessness predominated in Washington's recollection of how "late in the aftern[oo]n . . . the most tremendous rain that can be conceived" began to fall. The deluge "filled our trenches with water," he wrote; it "wet, not only the ammunition in Cartouch boxes and firelocks, but that which was in [the storehouse of the fort] . . . ; and left us with nothing but a few (for all were not provided with them) Bayonets for defence."[32]

With so many men dead and wounded and no functioning weapons left to defend those who survived, there had obviously been no choice but to accept the terms of surrender the French offered at the end of the day. Yet Washington felt the need to elaborate, explaining further the extremity of his circumstances: there had been "no Salt provisions" in the fort, he wrote, and little in the way of "fresh; which, from the heat of the weather, would not keep."[33] Even after drafting his version of the episode he returned to add a further reflection—one that suggests he continued to brood on this, his first great failure. His initial description of the onset of battle had made it clear that he knew, well in advance, of the enemy's overwhelming numerical advantage; his Indian scouts had seen the approaching force, he wrote, and immediately "resolved to retreat[,] as they advised us to do also."[34] So why had he chosen to give battle rather than make a strategic withdrawal? Turning the page on its side, Washington inserted his explanation in the left margin: retreat had been "impracticable without abandoning our Stores—Baggage—&ca as the horses which had brought them to this place had returned for Provision[s]."[35]

Washington took over two hundred words to describe the Battle of Fort Necessity, and he wrote his account with far greater urgency than the passages that immediately preceded and followed it. Throughout he referred to the Virginia Regiment as "we," abandoning his otherwise-distancing habit of referring to

"Just As They Occurred To The Memory . . ."

himself in the third person. This would seem to suggest a sense of shared peril, for he resumed speaking of his unit as "the Virginia Regiment" once the danger had passed: following the surrender, he wrote, the Regiment withdrew to Alexandria "to recruit, & get supplied with cloathing & necessar[ies] of which *they* stood much in need."[36]

Washington's description of the Battle of Fort Necessity deserves more than passing notice because it stands out in several ways from the more or less straightforward narration that brackets it. Moreover, the features that set it apart—the way in which Washington went on at length, using more vivid language, recollecting telling details, pausing to analyze causes, and shifting from third- to first-person narration—recurred on three other occasions in the memoir. He described Braddock's defeat and the Anglo-American retreat after the Battle of the Monongahela in nearly eight hundred words;[37] recounted in another passage of almost two hundred words his escape from an intended ambush in 1756; and wrote a nearly 300-word-long account of an episode from 1758 when two detachments of Virginia provincials, thinking they had encountered the enemy, opened fire on each other. Taken together, these four episodes comprise the dramatic heart of the memoir, and make up more than one third of its length.

That Washington took time and care in composing and revising the "Remarks" is evident from the emendations and additions he made to the manuscript. It would, therefore, seem reasonable to infer that these four events held some special significance for him in 1787, as he thought back over the occurrences of 1754–58. But what importance could they have had?

Certainly they were not necessary to a comprehensive narrative of the war's great events. The four acknowledged turning points in the French and Indian War on the Virginia-Pennsylvania frontier were the Battle of Fort Necessity, which inaugurated hostilities in the region; Braddock's expedition and defeat, which opened the Anglo-American backcountry to devastating guerrilla raids; the destruction of Fort Duquesne and the French withdrawal from the Forks of the Ohio in late 1758; and Britain's construction of Fort Pitt on the same site the following year, securing the region for the remainder of the war and restoring peace to the middle colonies' devastated frontier. In his "Remarks" Washington dealt with only the first two of these in detail, and referred to the seizure of the Forks of the Ohio in an aside: "the enemy dispairing of its [Fort Duquesne's] defence, blew it up—having first embarked their Artillery Stores & Troops—and retreated by

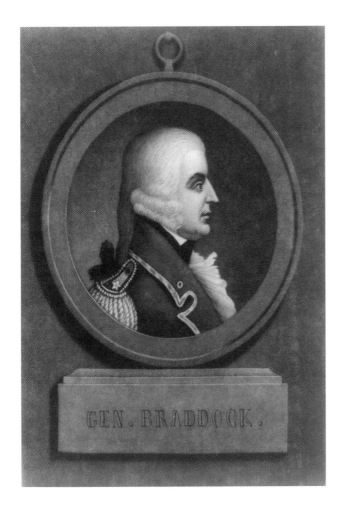

GEN. BRADDOCK.

"Just As They Occurred To The Memory . . ."

General Edward Braddock, John Sartain mezzotint, c.1850. Coldstream Guard officer Edward Braddock (1695–1755) was chosen to drive the French from Pennsylvania but instead found defeat and death only six miles from his Fort Duquesne goal in 1755. He was impressed by young George Washington who called him "brave and generous . . . but plain and blunt . . . even to rudeness." No portrait of the general from life has been found. (*Library of Congress, Washington, D.C.*)

water down the Ohio to their Settlements below."[38] He made no mention of the occupation of the Forks and the building of Fort Pitt.

Nor did his choice of events indicate any intent to cast himself as a hero or shaper of events. The experiences Washington chose to recount were predominantly failures: he lost his first battle, was helpless to prevent Braddock's defeat, could not keep Indian and French raiders from visiting havoc on the backcountry, and failed for years to persuade British generals and Virginia politicians that the only way to restore peace to the frontier was to mount an expedition against Fort Duquesne. Nor did he claim prowess in battle; if he ever killed an enemy, he made no mention of it. Indeed, when he referred to the physical experience of the war, instead of mentioning the strength and hardihood his contemporaries attributed to him, he described his weakness. Following his cursory mention of the French destruction of Fort Duquesne, for example, he described at greater length the reasons for his resignation from the service: his health had grown "precarious" after a long decline "occasioned by an inveterate disorder in his Bowels."[39] These problems with dysentery dated at least from the Braddock expedition, when he "mounted his horse on cushions" the day of the battle—presumably to cope with the pain of hemorrhoids.[40] Washington was frank in describing this illness, but then he was writing for Humphreys' eyes, not those of the public. That it was all more than faintly embarrassing would seem apparent from Humphreys' decision to convert the "inveterate disorder in his Bowels" into "an inveterate pulmonary complaint" when he wrote the final version of "The Life of General Washington."[41]

If his choice to linger on the four episodes reflected no consistent public purpose—and neither a desire to tell a comprehensive story of the war nor an intention to describe his own role in shaping the course of events would seem to explain it—the likeliest explanation is simply that they possessed a private significance for Washington, one that he did not feel called upon to explain. Because he did not elaborate, we can only speculate on why they mattered enough to evoke the extended treatment they did. One element they have in common, however, hints at what that significance might have been: all four are scenes in which Washington was in mortal danger, yet escaped without a scratch. All four, in other words, were episodes of personal deliverance.

Either directly or by inference, his descriptions of episodes made clear their perilous character. His account of the defeat at Fort Necessity stressed that at the end of the battle his command had no functioning weapons, no food, no hope of escape, and "a full third of our numbers . . . killed or wounded." Yet he had emerged unscathed. Similarly, in describing the Battle of the Monongahela, he pointed out that because Braddock's other two aides suffered incapacitating wounds, he "remained the sole aid through the day, to the Gen[era]l." Washington rode beside his chief until Braddock finally fell with a mortal wound after three hours under fire, by which time two-thirds of his men lay dead or wounded on the battlefield. Yet Washington, who "had one horse killed, and two wounded under him—A ball through his hat—and several through his clothes . . . escaped unhurt."[42]

On these two occasions he knew full well the danger of his situation, but Washington remained unaware that he had "narrowly escaped" death a third time until long after the fact. While on a tour of frontier forts in the autumn of 1756, he "and a small party of horse" passed over a section of road along which the enemy had prepared an ambush. As he learned afterward from "some of our People who were Prisoners with them," the Indians did not fire on him and his companions because their leader, expecting to waylay a group approaching from the opposite direction, had ordered them "not to take notice" of parties passing while he went off to "observe the number [and] manner of . . . movement" of "the prey they were in weight [wait] of." Thus, Washington wrote, "I passed & escaped alm[os]t certain destruction[,] for the weather was raining and the few Carbines [that our party carried would have been] unfit for use if we had escaped the first fire."[43]

The final episode occurred late on 12 November 1758 near Fort Ligonier, Pennsylvania, during the Forbes campaign. The French at Fort Duquesne, making last-ditch efforts to disrupt the approach of the Anglo-American army, created "a circumstance," Washington reported, "w[hi]ch involved the life of G.W. in as much jeopardy as it had ever been before or since."[44] In response to the reported presence of "a large detachment" of French and Indians sent out "to reconnoitre our Camp," Lieutenant Colonel George Mercer took 500 soldiers from the Second Virginia Regiment to engage the enemy. When firing erupted in the distance, Washington "called . . . for Volunteers and immediately marched at their head to sustain, as was conjectured[,] the retiring troops" of Mercer's party.[45] In the gloom of dusk, the two parties of Virginians collided and opened fire. One officer "& several privates were killed and many wounded before a stop could be put to it," Washington recalled; "to accomplish which G.W. never was in more imminent danger by being between two fires, knocking up with his sword the presented pieces."[46] What makes this particular recollection distinctive is that this was the only time Washington ever wrote about it.

Washington would not have taken the time and care he did to describe these four events if he had thought them inconsequential. He obviously found significance in the fact that when hundreds of men had been killed and injured, he had escaped with less damage to his person than he might have suffered in a bad morning's shave. In one sense, of course, this may only reflect the impulse, nearly universal among combat veterans, to tell stories about having cheated death. At a more specifically historical level, however, it may also be significant that Washington dwelt at such length on these four occasions of deliverance *when* he did, in late 1787 or early 1788, a point at which he was convinced that the future of the United States hung in the balance.

Here we move into the realm of speculation, for Washington did not choose to explain why he dwelt as he did on those four crucial episodes. Yet we do know a good deal, in general terms, about how he understood historical processes; indeed, in light of a large number of references in his writings, we even know something of how he thought of his own role as an actor on the histor-

"Just As They Occurred To The Memory . . ."

Plan of the Retrench'd Camp at Fort Ligonier, 1758.

Scale of 400 Feet

Road to Fort Bedford

1st Highland Battn.

1st Battn. Pensylvanians

Maryland, & Carolinians

2d Virginian Regt.

Hospital

Quar. Artillery

Guard Artillery

2d Battn. Pensylvanians

1st Virginian Regt.

Hospitals

Indian Camp

Bullock Penn

LOYAL HANNON CREEK

Indian Camp

858

J.C. Pleydell.

"Plan of the Retrench'd Camp at Fort Ligonier," 1758, by J.C. Pleydell. British General John Forbes designed a "protected advance" for his successful campaign to capture the Forks of the Ohio in 1758. At Fort Ligonier, erected on Loyalhanna Creek fifty miles from the redcoat goal and named for the commander of British forces, Colonel George Washington led provincial troops in and around the stockade, preparing for the final assault on Fort Dusquesne. *(The Royal Collection © 2003 Her Majesty Queen Elizabeth II)*

128

ical stage. And from these we may draw a few tentative inferences about the significance of the four critical events that George Washington remembered.

Like most other thoughtful western Europeans and Euro-Americans of his day, Washington subscribed to what we could call a "teleological" view of history. In philosophy, teleology is the doctrine that explains the universe in terms of a final cause, the character of which can be determined by studying the order (or design) that is apparent in it. The best-known example of this kind of reasoning in the eighteenth century was the extrapolation of a clockmaker-like Creator from the paths of planets that moved in sublime harmony with Newton's laws of motion and gravitation. Translated into historical terms, those who subscribed to the teleological world-view believed that human events also did not occur randomly, but worked toward some ultimate end. Like the motions of the planets, the action of electric charges, or the ordered hierarchies of plant and animal life, historical occurrences could be studied for evidences of God's character and purposes. Washington used a variety of terms, all more or less conventional in the eighteenth century, to describe this relatively impersonal divine power: the Author of the Universe, the Great Creator, the Ruler of Events, the Grand Architect, the Supreme Being, God. The term he preferred, however, was Providence.[47]

Washington's Providence was a generally benevolent, as well as an omnipotent, omnipresent, omniscient being, but He was hardly the kind of warm and loving God embraced by the evangelical Protestants whose numbers were growing fast in the post-war United States. Washington conceived of Him as a less personally concerned Deity than the evangelicals' God; His ultimate purpose was "to bring round the greatest degree of happiness to the greatest number of his people."[48] The comfort that Washington derived from his faith in the ordering power of Providence, therefore, had much less to do with the forgiveness of sins and the hope of eternal salvation than with the reassuring knowledge that a wisdom beyond human understanding lay behind everything that happened in the world. No matter how violent, bleak, or forbidding present circumstances seemed, everything would unfold according to a plan that human beings could only glimpse in part, but which was ultimately for the best.

This faith may seem an austere one, but Washington's repeated references to Providence in times of stress indicates that it was a very real help to him. In June 1775, for instance, he wrote a heartfelt letter to his wife just after the Continental Congress had

"Just As They Occurred To The Memory . . ."

appointed him commander in chief, explaining that he would be joining the army in Massachusetts rather than returning to Mount Vernon. He had hoped to avoid the appointment, he wrote, but in the end could not have declined it "without exposing my Character to such censures as would have reflected dishonour upon myself." Thus, he wrote, "as it has been a kind of destiny that has thrown me upon this Service, I shall hope that my undertaking of it, is design[e]d to answer some good purpose." Meanwhile, he continued,

> I shall rely . . . , confidently, on that Providence which has heretofore preserv[e]d, & been bountiful to me, not doubting that I shall return safe to you in the fall—I shall feel no pain from the Toil, or the danger of the Campaign—My unhappiness will flow, from the uneasiness I know you will feel at being left alone.[49]

Washington, of course, did not return home that fall, or any of the eight falls that followed it. To judge from his repeated appeals to Providence during those long years, it would seem that travail only deepened his confidence in the divine purpose that animated events, and his conviction that to live honorably one must fulfill whatever role God might ordain. As he explained his views to Humphreys in 1793, following the execution of Louis XVI,

> The rapidity of national revolutions appear[s] no less astonishing than their magnitude. In what they will terminate, is known only to the great ruler of events; and confiding in his wisdom and goodness, we may safely trust the issue to him, without perplexing ourselves to seek for that, which is beyond human ken; only taking care to perform the parts assigned us, in a way that reason and our own conscience approve of.[50]

Was this notion that Providence had spared his life for some purpose at the back of his mind as he described his four moments of deliverance in the "Remarks"? We cannot know, but two small pieces of evidence hint that something of the sort may have been the case. The first occurs in a letter that Washington wrote at New York on 20 July 1776, to the man who had been second-in-command of the Virginia Regiment, Adam Stephen. Even as Washington wrote, British troops were fortifying Staten Island and Royal Navy vessels were probing American defenses around

Manhattan. Yet with all that to worry about, Washington concluded his letter thus:

> I did not let the Anniversary of the 3d or 9th of this Inst[an]t [month] pass of[f] without a grateful remembrance of the escape we had at the Meadows and on the Banks of the Monongahela. [T]he same Provedence that protected us upon those occasions will, I hope, continue his Mercies, and make us happy Instruments in restoring Peace & liberty to this once favour'd, but now distressed Country.[51]

Clearly, then, Washington regarded two of the four crucial incidents in the "Remarks" as Providential events. They were significant enough to be remembered on the anniversaries of their occurrence, notwithstanding the pressure he faced as the British prepared to attack his army.

The second fragment of evidence is less direct, but still suggestive, for it has to do with the order in which Washington wrote about his narrow escapes from death. When he composed the section of the "Remarks" that dealt with the defense of the frontier in the aftermath of Braddock's defeat, he initially wrote only of the defenselessness of the backwoods settlers, and frustration at not being able to attack the root of the evil, Fort Duquesne. This was the passage as he originally wrote it:

> As G.W. foresaw, so it happened, the frontiers were continually harassed—but not having force enough to carry the war to the gates of Du Quesne, he could do no more than distribute the Troops along the Frontiers in Stockaded Forts; more with a view to quiet[ing] the fears of the Inhabitants than from any expectation of giving security to so extensive a line of settlements. Never ceasing in the mean time in his attempts, to demonstrate to the Legislature of Virg[ini]a—to Lord Loudoun—&ca that the only means of preventing the devastations to which the middle states were exposed, was to remove the cause.[52]

Together these sentences were perfectly coherent, brief, and to the point, for he used them to set up his account of events in 1758, when at last "an Expedition against Fort Du Quesne was concerted"—that is, the Forbes campaign, which expelled the French, restored peace to the backcountry, and thereby vindicated his earlier arguments.

It was in the course of describing the events of 1758 that Wash-

"Just As They Occurred To The Memory . . ."

ington paused to recount the terrifying moment when he found himself "in imminent danger by being between two fires, knocking up with his sword the presented pieces" of the Virginia provincials. He then concluded his story with quick descriptions of his resignation and the affectionate farewell his men had given him. This carried him to the bottom of the ninth page of his "Remarks."[53] The form of the manuscript suggests that it was at this point he turned back to re-read and edit the whole of the long passage—now covering eight pages—he had written.

As he reconsidered the text, other recollections and reflections evidently pressed in on him, for he began to crowd the margins of the earlier pages with additional thoughts, keyed to insertion points in the narrative. This was probably when interpolated his explanation of why he did not order a retreat from Fort Necessity; it is certainly the point at which he added a great deal to his account of the Battle of the Monongahela. Indeed, he had so much to say that he entirely filled the left-hand margin of page 7 and found he was still far from finished;[54] so he turned over the last sheet (on the front of which was his ninth page) and wrote a continuation that described a harrowing ride through the "impervious darkness" of the forest on the night following Braddock's defeat.[55] Having completed that addition he returned to his editing on page 8. There, in the midst of his short passage on frontier defense, he recalled his escape from the intended ambush near Fort Vause in 1756, and so inserted the story between the first and second sentences of the block quotation reprinted above.[56] Turning the page on its side, he filled the left margin, only to find that he had barely reached the halfway point of the tale; thus he turned once again to the back of page 9 to finish it. In the manuscript this continuation appears on the bottom half of the page, separated from the story of his night-long ride by three or so inches of blank space.[57]

In other words, what appears in the transcription of the "Remarks" as Washington's third episode of deliverance from death was actually the *fourth* one he composed, and he recalled it after writing his account of the friendly-fire incident and revising the story of Braddock's defeat—two more obvious instances in which he escaped death. This would seem to imply that by the time he had finished drafting his memoir Washington had become very much attuned to a pattern of deliverance in thinking about his life from 1754 through 1758. To a man as accustomed as he was to seeking evidence of Providential designs, the question would have been inescapable: for what purpose had his life been spared, not once but four times? Obviously, he had had a further role to play as the commander in chief of the Continental Army. But was that all?

In Washington's view, the United States at the end of 1787 was in greater peril than it had been since the darkest days of the war. Moreover, he knew full well that if the Constitution were ratified in the coming year he was almost certain to be offered the Presidency. He dreaded that possibility, even as he had dreaded the invitation to command the Army in 1775, for exactly the same reasons: reluctance to leave Mount Vernon and his family, fear of failure and loss of reputation, lack of confidence in his capacity for the tasks he would face. He also would have been intensely aware of the imperatives of honor and duty, which in 1775 had made it impossible to decline a part for which Providence had evidently chosen him. Had Independence been declared in 1776 and secured in 1783 only to be lost to the anarchic tendencies of the American people? Soon he would write to Lafayette that he

"Just As They Occurred To The Memory . . ."

"could not believe that Providence has done so much for nothing."[58] Yet if that were so, what new tasks might he be called upon to perform?

We have now traveled as far into the forest of speculation as any prudent historian would wish to go. Nonetheless, having ventured so far down the path, it would seem hard not to draw the final inference that even before Humphreys handed him the draft to correct, Washington had already begun, privately, to struggle with his sense of duty. If so, he had excellent reasons to examine the course of his extraordinary youth for evidences of design, and then—having discovered not just one or two but four successive instances of deliverance—excellent reasons to suspect that Providence might have spared his life not just to lead the Continental Army in the achievement of Independence, but also for further purposes, not yet been attained.

In that case Washington would have had cause to regard his "Remarks" not just as a series of recollections but as an examination of the trajectory of his life. Because such a meditation on pattern and purpose was essentially a private matter, it made perfect sense for him to ask "that the *whole* of what Is here contained may be returned to G.W. or committed to the flames," once Humphreys had separated its "grains . . . from the chaff." Washington knew that he had not composed a definitive or artful narrative, only a candid one. "Some of the enumerations are trifling," he wrote, "and perhaps more important circumstances omitted; but just as they occurred to the memory, they were committed." If the writing had indeed given him some perspective on his present position and future duty by disclosing a significant pattern in his earlier life, he would have understood his memoir as private and practical in character—and in that sense an exercise not wholly unlike keeping track of the weather in his diary. What he could not have suspected was that its very artlessness would be what gives his memoir such value, and such emotional power, today. After two centuries' time, the "Remarks" allows us, as no other document he ever wrote could, to glimpse the meaning of his French and Indian War experiences through George Washington's mature eyes, as he pondered their significance in a life story that was still far from complete.

NOTES

1. The massive editorial and publishing project known as *The Papers of George Washington* began in 1969 at the University of Virginia; it is still in progress. The edition of six thematic and chronological series began to appear in 1976 with *The Diaries of George Washington*, edited by Donald Jackson and Dorothy Twohig; these six volumes, the publication of which was completed in 1979, were followed by the official extension of his diaries, *The Journal of the Proceedings of the President, 1793–1797* (1981), and by a one-volume abridgement in 1999. *The Papers of George Washington* proper began publication in 1983 with the ten volumes of the *Colonial Series*, under the general editorship of W. W. Abbot. Subsequent divisions have continued to appear ever since: the *Revolutionary War Series* (beginning in 1985, and still in progress under the general editorship of Philander D. Chase; twelve volumes to date), the *Confederation Series* (complete in six volumes, published between 1992 and 1997), the *Presidential Series* (starting in 1987, and continuing under Chase's editorship; eleven volumes to date), and the *Retirement Series* (completed in four volumes under the general editorship of Dorothy Twohig and published in 1998–99). Fifty-one letterpress volumes have appeared thus far. Perhaps forty remain to be published. By comparison, the most nearly comprehensive previous edition, *The Writings of George Washington*, edited by John C. Fitzpatrick for the Library of Congress and published by the U.S. Government Printing Office between 1931 and 1939, had thirty-nine volumes.

2. Dorothy Twohig, ed., *George Washington's Diaries: An Abridgement* (Charlottesville, Va., 1999), quotation at 428.

3. Washington to James McHenry, 29 July 1798, in Dorothy Twohig et al, eds., *The Papers of George Washington, Retirement Series*, Vol. 2, *January–September 1798* (Charlottesville, Va., 1998), 473.

4. "Preface" to W. W. Abbot, ed., *The Papers of George Washington, Colonial Series*, Vol. 1, *1748–August 1755* (Charlottesville, Va., 1983), xvii–xviii. Washington apparently intended his alterations as instructions to a scribe engaged to make a fair copy of his earliest letter-books; the intent was evidently not to distort his earlier writings, but to correct what he believed were inelegant or imprecise expressions of his intended meaning. The first volume of the *Washington Papers* reproduces these alterations throughout. They do not, generally, change the content of his earlier texts. For the context of Washington's concern with his reputation (which paralleled that of virtually all of his Revolutionary contemporaries) see Douglass Adair, "Fame and the Founding Fathers," in Trevor Colbourne, ed., *Fame and the Founding Fathers: Essays by Douglass Adair* (New York, 1974), 3–26; also (among many other biographies) see Paul K. Longmore, *The Invention of George Washington* (Berkeley, Calif., 1988), esp. 1–16, 46–67, 160–211.

5. See George Washington, "Remarks," War for Empire, Inc. Pitts-

"Just As They Occurred To The Memory . . ."

burgh, 13 (hereinafter referred to as "Remarks." The page numbers refer to the facsimile in this volume.) See transcript above, 24.

6. Rosemarie Zagarri, ed., *David Humphreys' "Life of General Washington" with George Washington's "Remarks"* (Athens, Ga., 1991), xviii–xix; idem. "Biography and Autobiography: Washington's 'Remarks' in Context," above, 88.

7. W. W. Abbot, "Comments on David Humphreys' Biography of George Washington: Editorial Note," in Dorothy Twohig et al., eds., *The Papers of George Washington, Confederation Series,* Vol. 5, *February–December 1787* (Charlottesville, Va., 1997), 514–15. The editors' judgment accords generally with the careful findings of Rosemarie Zagarri in *Humphreys' "Washington,"* xxi.

8. Among other treatments of Washington as a modern counterpart to the Roman hero, see esp. Garry Wills, *Cincinnatus: George Washington and the Enlightenment* (Garden City, N. Y., 1984).

9. Douglas Southall Freeman, *George Washington: A Biography,* Vol. 6, *Patriot and President* (New York, 1954), 4, 14; Memorandum to George McCarmick, 12 July 1784, in W. W. Abbot and Dorothy Twohig, eds., *The Papers of George Washington, Confederation Series,* Vol. 1, *January–July 1784* (Charlottesville, Va., 1992), 500–01; Robert F. Dalzell, Jr., and Lee Baldwin Dalzell, *Washington's Mount Vernon: At Home in Revolutionary America* (New York, 1998), 181–87.

10. Washington's correspondence with Bataille Muse, the agent he employed from 1784 for rent-collection on his western lands, is full of vexation over the difficulty of evicting squatters, the inability to make tenants pay, the flight of debtors, the uncooperativeness of sheriffs, and the shortage of usable coin. See, e.g., Muse to Washington, 4 February 1787, and Washington to Muse, 14 February 1787, in *Papers of Washington, Confederation Ser.,* 5: 11–13, 30.

11. Freeman, *Washington,* 6: 144–45.

12. "Never Lived soe pore": Mary Ball Washington to John Augustine Washington, January 1787, quoted in *Papers of Washington, Confederation Ser.,* 5: 36n.1; other quotations: Washington to Mary Ball Washington, 15 February 1787, ibid., 33.

13. Washington had first written to Young in the last half of 1786. See especially Young's reply of 1 February 1787, ibid., 3–6, which accompanied a set of improved plows, four bushels of wheat seed, and advice on building a new-modeled barn.

14. For the best concise treatment of Washington's ideas and activities concerning transportation links to the West, their larger significance, and their context, see John Lauritz Larson, *Internal Improvement: National Public Works and the Promise of Popular Government in the Early United States* (Chapel Hill, N.C., 2001), 10–20.

15. Washington's reluctant but principled participation in the writing of the Constitution is treated in every Washington biography and

virtually every account of the Convention. For an able conventional summary, see Freeman, *Washington,* 6: 68–116; cf. the more exuberant argument in Wills, *Cincinnatus,* 151–172.

16. *Papers of Washington, Confederation Ser.,* 5: 333–514 passim; Freeman, *Washington,* 6: 130–34.

17. Benjamin Rush to Timothy Pickering, 30 August 1787: "The new federal government like a new Continental waggon will overset our State dung cart. . . . From the conversations of the Members of the Convention, there is reason to believe the foederal Constitution will be wise—vigorous—safe—free—& full of Dignity. —General Washington it is said will be placed at the head of the new Government, or in the stile of my simile, will drive the new waggon." Max Farrand, ed., *The Records of the Federal Convention of 1787,* rev. ed., Vol. 4 (New Haven, Conn., 1937), 75.

18. See the objections he later raised to accepting the office for a sense of his scruples; e.g., Washington's letters to Alexander Hamilton (28 August 1788) and Henry Lee, Jr. (22 September 1788), in Dorothy Twohig, ed., *The Papers of George Washington, Confederation Series,* Vol. 6, *January–September 1788* (Charlottesville, Va., 1997), 480–81, 528–31.

19. *Humphreys' "Washington,"* 9.

20. Ibid., 10.

21. Washington does not mention here that the name had initially been bestowed on his great-grandfather, Colonel John Washington, in recognition of his propensity for destroying Doeg and other Indian settlements during the Susquehannock War. "Caunotocarious" in that context meant "devourer of villages" and was therefore no more a compliment than a modern Bosnian villager would intend if he called a Serbian paramilitary commander by the same title. Washington, no doubt thinking in terms of one who captured fortified European towns according to the civilized procedures of eighteenth-century siege warfare, imagined that the title connoted valor. He remained unaware that to the Indians it bespoke the savage ruthlessness of what today would be called "ethnic cleansing." On the word's original meaning, see *Papers of Washington, Col. Ser.* 1: 91n.8.

Ironically, Washington may have suggested the title himself. The Half-King, Tanaghrisson, whom he said bestowed the sobriquet, was a Seneca chief sent by the Iroquois League Council to oversee the Indians—Delawares, Shawnees, Mingos, and other Iroquois client groups—who lived near the Forks of the Ohio. Tanaghrisson was a Catawba by birth; in boyhood he had been taken captive along with his mother and then adopted into the Seneca nation. It is hard (although not quite impossible) to imagine John Washington's destruction of Doeg, Conoy, and Susquehannock villages in northern Virginia during the 1670s was sufficiently well-known among the Senecas of New York

"Just As They Occurred To The Memory . . ."

eighty years later that Tanaghrisson would make the connection between the original Caunotocarious and his great-grandson without at least some prompting. If the name had passed down the generations as family lore among the Washingtons, however, there is every reason to imagine that the ghastly title "devourer of villages" would have been transmuted, over time, into the more glorious "Town Taker." In this light it seems entirely plausible that Washington, a novice in Indian diplomacy, could have told Tanaghrisson of his ancestor's *nom de guerre* in an effort to impress him with the warlike stuff that the Washingtons were made of.

The name Caunotocarious stuck to Washington among the Iroquois during the Revolutionary period as a result of the Continental Army's phenomenally destructive invasion of their homeland in the Sullivan Expedition of August and September 1779. In this episode, which comes as close to ethnic cleansing as anything in American history, the soldiers of Washington's Continental Army destroyed 40 towns and killed as many Indian men, women, and children as they could catch. By the end of the campaign—in total disregard, it must be said, of Washington's explicit orders—not a single Indian had been taken prisoner. All but a comparatively small number of Oneidas, who had sided with the United States at the outset of the war, had been made refugees. The survivors of General Sullivan's onslaught lived for the remainder of the war in Ontario, under the protection of the British garrison at Niagara, whence they raided the colonists of upstate New York with redoubled fury.

The Hodenosaunee (Iroquois) people refer to the President of the United States by Washington's old sobriquet, Caunotocarious, to this day.

22. *Humphreys' "Washington,"* 10.

23. Ibid., 22–24. Humphreys' papers were broken up after his death, and it is impossible to speak of a definitive final version of the "Life." According to Rosemarie Zagarri, the closest student of the fragmented manuscripts that make up the Humphreys biography, Washington was commenting on the second signature of a manuscript now held by the Rosenbach Museum and Library in Philadelphia (ibid., xxiii, xxvi). In the 600-word passage cited above, she has combined a brief passage from a second manuscript, held in the Humphreys-Marvin-Olmsted Collection at Yale University, with a longer section drawn from the Rosenbach document. Phrases in the Yale manuscript that strongly echo Washington's suggest that Humphreys composed it after he had read the "Remarks." The omission from the Yale document of any mention of Washington's skirmish with Ensign Jumonville (28 May 1754) or of his defeat at Fort Necessity (3 July 1754), therefore, would seem to suggest that Humphreys' ultimate intent was to minimize the amount of coverage given to the origins of the French and Indian War, and indeed to the war generally. This is, of course, perfectly under-

standable: so far as Humphreys and his contemporaries were concerned, it went without saying that the main event in Washington's life was the Revolutionary War; the earlier conflict, so replete with failure and defeat for his hero, was no more than a prologue. The far greater attention Washington gave to describing his experiences in the French and Indian War, however, argues that he did not necessarily share Humphreys' view.

24. "Remarks," 3. See transcript above, 16.

25. Ibid., 4, 11. See transcript above, 16, 23.

26. Ibid., 4. See transcript above, 16–17.

27. The officer who commanded the independent company was James Mackay, and Washington's opinion of him had mellowed considerably since 1754, when Mackay had arrived at Fort Necessity with "none of the Cannon" that Washington had understood he was to bring, "very little Ammunition, ab[ou]t 5 Days allowance of flower, and 60 Beeves." Worse, Mackay both refused to order his men to work on the road alongside the Virginia troops and insisted that his royal commission as a captain superseded Washington's provincial commission as a lieutenant colonel. Washington refused to recognize Mackay's authority, which would in effect have given him command of the Virginia Regiment, and appealed to Lieutenant Governor Robert Dinwiddie of Virginia to settle the issue and prevent "the Evil tendancy that will accompany Capt[ai]n McKays com[mandin]g for I am sorry to observe this is what we always hop'd to enjoy—the Rank of Officers which to me Sir is much dearer than the Pay." Washington to Dinwiddie, [10 June 1754], *Papers of Washington, Col. Ser.*, 1: 129–38 (quotations at 138). In the end the question of who commanded at Fort Necessity was never settled, and the two forces operated separately.

28. "Remarks," 5. See transcript above, 17.

29. For a more detailed account of this episode, see Fred Anderson, *Crucible of War: The Seven Years' War and the Fate of Empire in British North America, 1754–1766* (New York, 2000), 5–7, 52–59.

30. Don Higginbotham, "Young Washington: Ambition, Accomplishment, and Acclaim," above, 75–76.

31. "Remarks," 5. See transcript above, 17–18.

32. Ibid.

33. Ibid.

34. Ibid.

35. Ibid. See left margin on "Remarks," 5.

36. Ibid, 6. See transcript above, 18.

37. The account of Braddock's defeat and its aftermath conforms to the pattern described here in every way but one: he does not shift out of his exclusive use of the third person in narrating it. This would seem to suggest that while he obviously saw himself in danger at the Battle of the Monongahela, he distanced himself in memory from the other participants in ways he did not in the other three episodes. The likeliest expla-

"Just As They Occurred To The Memory . . ."

nation would seem to be related to a shift in political and cultural identity. In each of the three other cases, Washington was himself in command of provincial soldiers, most of whom were Virginians. Here the force being attacked was made up principally of British regulars, under a British commander. While Washington had been more than willing to identify himself with them in 1755, the intervening decades had obviously led him to make critical distinctions between Britons and Americans. By the time he wrote in 1787, the change in his national self-identification may have prevented him from using the first-person plural to describe the group with whom he had shared such mortal peril, three decades before.

38. "Remarks," 11. See transcript above, 23.

39. Ibid.

40. Ibid., 7. See transcript above, 19.

41. *Humphreys' "Washington,"* 24.

42. "Remarks," 8. See transcript above, 20.

43. Ibid., 10. See transcript above, 22. Although Washington does not date this episode, his mention that it occurred "near Fort Vass" dates it to a tour of the southwestern frontier of Virginia he conducted in the fall of 1756; he visited Fort Vause on about 8 October. See Douglas Southall Freeman, *George Washington: A Biography*, Vol. 2, *Young Washington* (New York, 1948), 216–18. Freeman notes that Washington's party consisted only of himself, a servant, and a guide. The party approaching from the opposite direction consisted of two men, one of whom was killed, and the other taken prisoner.

44. "Remarks," 10. See transcript above, 23.

45. Ibid., 11. See transcript above, 23.

46. Ibid. Because Washington did not date this episode in his "Remarks" and never mentioned it in any of his correspondence, the date can be fixed only by reference to Gen. John Forbes's report to the commander in chief. See Forbes to James Abercromby, 17 November 1758, in Alfred Procter James, ed., *Writings of General John Forbes Relating to His Service in North America* (Menasha, Wis., 1938), 255–56; also Freeman, *Washington*, 2: 357–58; and Anderson, *Crucible*, 282. In fact casualties were higher than Washington suggested in the "Remarks"; two officers and 38 men were killed or wounded in the exchange of fire.

47. Paul F. Boller, Jr., *George Washington and Religion* (Dallas, Tex., 1963), 94. The following discussion derives principally from Chapter V, "Washington's Religious Opinions," 92–115. For a more recent account of Washington's religious views, see Peter Henriques and Philander Chase, *The Death of George Washington: He Died as He had Lived* (Charlottesville, Va., 2002).

48. Washington to Jonathan Trumbull, 6 September 1778, quoted in Boller, *Washington and Religion*, 96.

49. Washington to Martha Washington, 18 June 1775, in W. W. Abbot et al., eds., *The Papers of George Washington, Revolutionary War*

Series, Vol. 1, *June–September 1775* (Charlottesville, Va., 1985), 4. This is one of only two private letters from Washington to his wife that survived her destruction of the correspondence in 1802, and thus offers a rare glimpse of the affectionate side of his personality.

50. Washington to Humphreys, 23 March 1793, quoted in Boller, *Washington and Religion,* 96.

51. Washington to Stephen, 20 July 1776, *Papers of Washington, Rev. Ser.* 5: 408–09.

52. "Remarks," 10. See transcript above, 22.

53. Ibid., 11.

54. Ibid., 9.

55. Ibid., 12.

56. Ibid., 10.

57. Ibid., 12.

58. Washington to Lafayette, 18 June 1788, *Papers of Washington, Confederation Ser.,* 6: 388. "It has always been my creed," he continued, "that we [Americans] should not be left as an awful monument to prove, 'that Mankind, under the most favourable circumstances of civil liberty and happiness, are unequal to the task of Governing themselves, and therefore made for a Master.'"

"Just As They Occurred To The Memory . . ."

Christine Smith

The Manuscript as Object

Appendix 1

ITS MATERIALS AND CONSERVATION

CONSERVATORS engage objects from a different perspective than historians or curators, generally focusing on three successive concerns: how an object was made, how it has aged, and how it should be repaired. Studying its materials and fabrication techniques, the conservator asks how they are affecting the object's longevity? Have poor quality materials degraded? Are incompatible materials working against each other? How has the environment affected the object? Has previous treatment changed it? How does the object's condition restrict the degree to which it should be used in the future?

Answers to those questions lead the conservator to sketch a preliminary treatment strategy, which will be refined by testing the object to learn whether it can tolerate certain procedures and whether it would benefit sufficiently to justify hazards inherent in each step. Mindful that the first rule of responsible conservation is to do no harm, the conservator considers whether hazards can be eliminated or lessened by modifying technique. Are there new materials, methods, or research projects that should be considered? What are the advantages and disadvantages of the various possibilities? Since conservation is a constantly evolving profession, would it be wiser to delay certain procedures until there is more research to support their use?

As the conservator works in a circular fashion to incorporate information provided by the object, research, and evolving ideas about exactly how to proceed, the strategy becomes increasingly specific. The final proposal is likely to address the object's immediate problems and make recommendations for storage and exhibition.

MATERIALS

The Paper

George Washington wrote his "Remarks" on three folios, a folio being a sheet of paper folded in half vertically to create four pages. Each page measures 12 5/8+" (32 cm) high by approximately 7 7/8" (20 cm) wide; and, except for a blank final page, writing covers both sides of all the leaves. The double-sided writing has affected the manuscript's appearance, deterioration, and conservation treatment.

Paper is made with innumerable variations, but in the western world some major distinctions include whether a sheet is handmade or machine-made, of high or poor quality (sometimes correlating to intention for long-term or temporary use), and the presence or absence of added decorative or functional treatments (e.g., coloring, embossing, or coating). The "Remarks" were written on handmade paper: the world's first patent application for a papermaking machine would not be filed until 1798, in Paris, and the first American machine would not begin operation until 1817, near Wilmington, Delaware. This is a high quality, general purpose writing paper, cream color with a gray or greenish cast. It is evenly formed except for a spot at the lower left of page 6, and the strong flax/linen and hemp fibers[1] and chemical-free processing have helped to preserve the manuscript despite deterioration of its ink. Intended for routine functions, it was given no ornament or additional treatment.

Papers are also classified as either "laid" or "wove," references to the type of screen on which the sheet was formed. The older "laid" screen consists of closely spaced horizontal wires, which give it firmness, and more widely spaced vertical wires, which hold the horizontal wires in position. Where screen wires block the fiber-water mixture from draining, less pulp is deposited; and these variations are visible in transmitted light. "Wove" screens, which were introduced to the United States *circa* 1788,[2] were

LAID PAPER WITH WATERMARK. In transmitted light, John Lungren's watermark, ILG, stands out on a background of horizontal laid lines and vertical chain lines. (The watermark is visible, in reverse, at the center of this image.) The watermark and laid and chain lines were created by wires on the papermaking screen.

WOVE PAPER. In transmitted light, the wrapper in which the Humphreys family stored the manuscript reveals the even fiber distribution of wove paper. This paper has no watermark.

developed to provide a more even paper surface. These screens are woven on a loom with thin wires, so the pulp drains with evenly distributed fibers.

A watermark is the papermaker's sign or logo. Made by sewing a wire design to the mould screen, it can be useful in dating and identifying the mill where a sheet was made. Transmitted light reveals that all the folios are marked with the initials ILG, representing John Lungren (also spelled Lum Gren, Lumgren, Longren), who owned and operated a mill on Ridley Creek, Upper Providence township in Delaware County, Pennsylvania between April 20, 1785 and December 1795.[3] So this paper, on which George Washington described events that occurred in western Pennsylvania, was made in that same state.

The Ink

A UBIQUITOUS MATERIAL   The manuscript was written with iron gall ink, the most commonly used writing ink in the western world during the 18th century. In fact, because this ink bites deeply into the paper or parchment below it—making alterations difficult—iron gall ink was the dominant ink for record writing from the 14th through the late 19th century in the West. In addition to Washington manuscripts, we are surrounded by objects made with this complex and problematic material: drawings by artists as varied as Rembrandt van Rijn and Vincent van Gogh, musical scores by J.S. Bach, Pennsylvania German fraktur (documents such as birth and wedding certificates, made with "fractured" gothic-style writing and folk art images), and letters from Civil War soldiers. Even typewriter inks were made with it.[4] Its ubiquity and generally auto-degrading character make this kind of ink of particular interest and concern to those who care for paper-based artifacts.

The Romans used the black liquid produced by the chemical reaction between tannic acid (from various plant materials) and ferrous sulfate (from iron) as shoe blacking,[5] and the Japanese used it to black their teeth;[6] but the material was not used as an ink until sometime in the 11th century.[7] During the 14th century it became the most common Western writing ink, almost certainly because its predecessor, which was made with carbon pigment and gum binder, could not adhere to parchment's greasy surface and therefore could be easily altered or eradicated. Besides the potential for alteration, carbon ink was vulnerable to smudging, sticking, and off-setting in a humid environment, such as the pages of a closed manuscript. Finally, grinding carbon particles to a uniform and appropriate size and suspending them in writing fluid required considerable skill.

In contrast, iron gall ink could be made easily from a range of materials that were readily available. Because it stained into the writing surface, rather than sitting on top, it was difficult to eradicate and resisted smudging. For these reasons it continued to be used as paper joined and then supplanted parchment as the usual writing surface. Iron gall inks predominated until about 1860, when aniline dyes brought radical changes to ink manufacture. Nevertheless, as late as 1940 a treatise on inks asserted, "This kind of ink is still used in larger quantities than any other."[8] Even today some calligraphers are attracted to the very sharp, fine, deep black lines it can make.

INGREDIENTS AND PREPARATION   "Iron gall ink" is really a generic term that can be applied to a large range of inks, and historic recipes were sometimes imprecise about quantities of ingredients or preparation techniques. In addition, its plant-based ingredients varied depending on the time of year, soil conditions, and plant species; and materials mined from the earth occurred in variable concentrations and often contained reactive impurities. Even the material from which the preparation vessel was made and the interval between making and using the ink influenced the product.

Nevertheless, all iron gall ink requires four essential ingredients: source materials for gallotannic acid and ferrous sulfate, vegetable gum binder, and water. Gallotannic acid is found in plant galls, which are growths that some trees (especially oaks) produce in response to the irritation of wasp eggs laid beneath the bark. Lesser concentrations of the acid occur in certain woods, leaves, fruits, and barks. The acid can be extracted in several ways: by crushing the galls and mixing them with water, by boiling them for several hours, by fermentation for several days, or by some combination of those methods. The ferrous sulfate, which was known by an assortment of names such as iron sulfate, vitriol, or copperas, was mined directly or dehydrated from water that ran through mine shafts. The most commonly used binding agent was gum arabic, which would have been purchased from an apothecary or other shop. Water might be gathered from rain or pumped. If beer or wine were used instead, there would be fewer potentially problematic impurities and the ink would contain alcohol, which provided resistance to fungal growth and freezing.

Mixing gallic or tannic acid[9] with an iron salt produces a water-soluble compound which penetrates the paper surface. With exposure to oxygen in the air, a water-insoluble pigment forms. A small amount of this pigment forms in the ink water, but much more is produced after the ink has been used and the writing or drawing is exposed to air for several days. The black pigment has a variable composition and is called ferric tannate, ferric gallotannate, ferrogallotannate or ferrotannate.

Water serves as the liquid carrier for the pigmenting materials. The gum acts in several ways: it suspends the pigment particles, modifies viscosity, and provides gloss and a deeper color. By briefly delaying the ink on top of the paper surface, the gum prevents soft-edged ink lines.

Additional ingredients were often added to the ink mixture, the most common being temporary coloring agents that made the ink legible before the gallotannic acid and ferrous sulfate reacted with the air. Indigo, carbon, and aniline dyes were among the materials used. Vinegar or other acidifiers were used to prevent premature precipitation of the ink complex. Honey or sugar slowed drying and heightened gloss. Mold inhibitors included vinegar, alcohol, cloves, alum salts, and common salt. Alcohol helped the ink to flow by reducing surface tension.

The particular ink that Washington used for writing the "Remarks" may have been imported from England, purchased in the port of Alexandria near his home, or prepared on one of his five farms. The width of the writing strokes varies from extraordinarily thin to fairly broad, suggesting that he used more than one quill pen over the course of his commenting, that he pressed into the paper to different degrees, or both. By visual examination it is not possible to determine whether the "Remarks" were written in one sitting or several, although the overall length of the manuscript and the number of revisions suggest that Washington did not write it all at once. Unfortunately neither materials analysis nor forensic analysis could be expected to clarify this question since any differences in the ink(s) would be too minimal to be meaningful.[10]

DETERIORATION   The ratio of gallotannic acid to ferrous sulfate is critical to the stability of an iron gall ink and because the odds are against a balanced formulation for a recipe with so many variables, many iron gall inks are unstable and degrade over time. Too much acid catalyzes deterioration by hydrolysis and may cause the ink to fade, sometimes nearly to invisibility. Too much ferrous sulfate catalyzes deterioration by oxidation and may cause

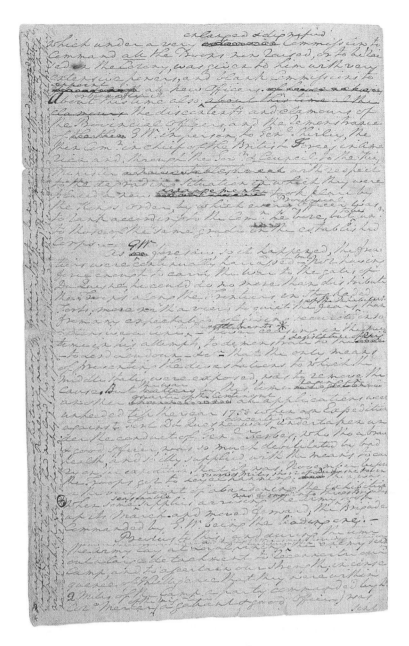

VARIABLE INK COLORS. New good quality iron gall ink is a rich bluish-black in color. The "Remarks" ink is not chemically stable and has aged to various shades of reddish-brown. Additions and corrections are now darker than the ink used for the body of the text; and even within the original text, the ink color varies.

the ink to break the paper beneath it.[11] The destructive hydrolysis and oxidation reactions complement and regenerate each other in an ongoing cycle.

As iron gall inks deteriorate, they pass through recognizable stages.[12] Initially, degradation is visible only as fluorescence in near-range ultraviolet radiation. Later symptoms can be seen in visible-range light. Brown halos develop just outside heavily inked areas, eventually breaks develop in the ink lines, and then areas of ink and paper fall out from the document, leaving holes in the paper.

Color change also may signal an ink's degradation. Fresh good quality iron gall ink is a velvety bluish black. The "Remarks" ink now ranges from pale to fairly dark reddish-brown. How much these color variations are due to differences in hand pressure, refilling the quill pen, or dilution is unclear. Brown halos are evi-

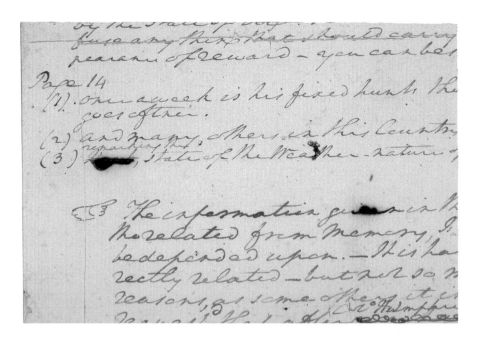

DEGRADATION HALOS. Just beyond the heavily inked areas, brown halos characteristic of the second stage of iron gall ink deterioration are visible. A break through the ink is visible in the upper splotch.

STAIN MIGRATION. Degradation products create stains that move from the ink through the body of the paper. Stained areas are weakened as well as discolored.

dent beyond the heavily inked areas, and staining has migrated to the opposite side of the paper in numerous areas. Transmitted light reveals that a few heavily inked lines have broken, and there are a few areas where bits of ink and paper have fallen out.

Recently a simple, yet sensitive, test was developed to detect unstable iron gall ink ions.[13] Paper test strips impregnated with a color indicator are moistened and held in contact with the ink. Unstable iron ions will move through the moisture and color the test paper. The "Remarks" ink was tested at four locations on every sheet and gave positive results on all of them. This corroborates the visual evidence that this particular ink is chemically unstable.

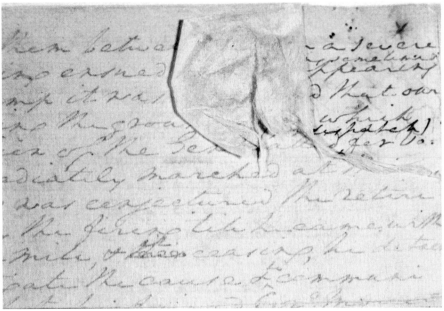

TISSUE OVERLAYS   At some time before November 1988 someone adhered medium weight tissue over one side of each sheet, using a starch paste.[14] Judging by the relative cleanliness of the tissue and its character (conservation grade Japanese paper that has been generally available in the United States only since the second half of the 20th century), this treatment may have been done as the Humphreys' family foundation prepared to sell the "Remarks" in 1974.

The tissue layer was applied to stabilize long splits in the manuscript: vertically along the folio folds and horizontally where the folios had been folded into thirds for storage, presumably by David Humphreys or his descendants, who made a small paper wrapper for the manuscript. Although the tissue did prevent splits and tears from growing longer and held weakened ink passages in situ, the facings seriously obscured fifty percent of the manuscript since it is written on both sides of the sheets. Fortunately the adhesive is readily soluble in water, enabling both the tissue and adhesive to be removed.

CONSERVATION

The unstable ink and obscuring tissue layers were major indicators that it was important to develop a treatment strategy. Additional conditions that called for treatment were the splits, tears, and small areas of loss: when the tissue overlays were removed, all those vulnerabilities would be fully exposed. The manuscript was lightly soiled, and the old, inscribed wrapper was quite dirty. The wrapper also had been lined with tissue and was overly stiffened by the process.

Designing a Treatment Protocol

The manuscript paper on which the "Remarks" were written is of high quality and it appeared to be in good condition—though sensing its flexibility and strength was impeded by the overlays. Thus, the concerns that guided development of a treatment protocol were focused on the ink and the method for housing the folios after treatment was complete.

The obvious need was to remove the tissue overlays. Tests indicated that with brief exposure to moisture they could be peeled from the manuscript without disrupting the paper surface, causing the ink to spread or change color, or aggravating splits and tears. Conservators bring paper and water together in many ways including immersion, floating, spraying, and humidification in a sealed chamber. The water's action may be modified by the addition of other chemicals, such as an alcohol to reduce surface tension at the object-solvent interface. Exposure periods may be varied at different points in treating the same object. To determine the best option(s) for the "Remarks," the advantages and disadvantages of each application method had to be weighed.

Because the adhesive was readily soluble, there was no need to test the safety of exposing the ink to large amounts of water. Brief, minimal contact would be sufficient. This was good news because iron gall inks sometimes contain excess or insufficiently bound pigment, and moisture can cause it to spread laterally, sink into the paper, or float away from the object altogether. Moreover, water can move provisional colorants since they may remain soluble long after the insoluble black pigment has formed.

However, current thinking is that an iron gall ink object should be treated either without water or with full flushing.[15] Recent research indicates that limited exposure to water can cause destructive iron ions to move out from the ink lines and increase an object's vulnerability to further chemical damage. Also, adhesive between the overlays and the manuscript had to be removed; and at that point in the treatment, water-soluble degradation products would create stains if they were not wetted evenly. And why just prevent stains? Better to purge the degradation products. Therefore, although only limited exposure to moisture was necessary to peel away the tissues, in fact we would have to find a safe way to expose the manuscript to considerably more water.

Further tests indicated that water could be applied to and through the manuscript without visible alteration to the ink. This suggested a variety of washing methods to remove paste residues, soluble iron ions, and other degradation products. However, as with so many other kinds of endeavors, in conservation practice objects do not always behave in the way tests predict. Therefore, while tests indicated that there was latitude in applying water, constant vigilance would be especially important for a manuscript that may have been written over a period of time in somewhat different inks.

After paper objects have been washed, conservators often apply sizing to the surface or through the cross-section of a sheet. Analogous to an extremely dilute adhesive coating, sizing serves a variety of purposes. It helps to restore the original surface appearance of a sheet, protect the fibers against dust, toughen the sheet, and prepare the surface for mending. In the Occident, the traditional sizing material has been gelatin, although a range of synthetic materials also are used now. For iron gall ink objects, gelatin sizing provides an additional benefit. It slightly complexes or inactivates iron ions, thereby helping to slow the rate at which the ink degrades the paper below it.[16]

On the "Remarks" manuscript, splits, tears, abrasions, and areas where the paper has been embrittled by the ink had to be reinforced without preventing the folios from opening and closing and without visual disturbance to the double-sided writing. On another Washington manuscript, similar problems were addressed by applying dilute washes of acrylic paint to an extremely sheer, but proportionally strong, tissue.[17] The acrylic binder toughened the tissue, allowing mending strips to be

Appendix 1

THE MANUSCRIPT

AS OBJECT

manipulated while wet with paste and later increasing their dry strength. Slightly coloring the translucent tissue helped it to blend with the tones of the underlying manuscript, producing nearly invisible mends. Paper conservators use a wide range of adhesives, but the standard is wheat starch paste. Among many virtues, it provides strength while remaining reversible and with-standing discoloration. For an object with long split lines, it is important that the adhesive be adjusted to balance the object's own strength, which may vary from area to area. This can be done by mixing in a weaker, albeit archival quality, adhesive and by using relatively shorter mending strips to distribute stresses over the sheet.

Because iron gall inks vary in the proportions of their ingredients, they often contain excess (chemically unbound) ferrous sulfate or gallotannic acid. This imbalance stimulates a cycle of two degradation processes, hydrolysis and oxidation, both of which must be stopped to stabilize the ink. Hydrolysis is halted by washing the object and then inserting an alkaline material to counteract excess acid content. When objects cannot tolerate washing, it is more difficult for the conservator to interrupt hydrolysis, but fortunately, the "Remarks" could be washed and given an alkaline buffer.

Oxidation is considered the more destructive reaction, but an apparently successful intervention has been developed recently.[18] A compound called calcium phytate is put into the paper to chemically "lock up" the iron ions, and thus block further oxidation. This procedure can be done easily and in combination with a treatment for hydrolysis should stabilize a vulnerable ink. Unfortunately for an object as important as the "Remarks," the treatment is too new to have been evaluated over a long period of natural aging, and there are always differences between the ways objects age under natural and artificial conditions. So the conservator faces a dilemma: Is it more responsible to bypass a new treatment which seems able to stabilize a clearly unstable ink because the procedure is not yet fully proven, or is it better to take action against the object's instability?

The last major step in the treatment was devising a housing format that serves the character and needs of the manuscript while accommodating the different institutions where it will be exhibited. To preserve its character, the document needs to retain its format as three folios. To allow the object to be displayed in environments that range from museums to historic forts and to enable staff members to handle the manuscript safely and with

confidence, both paper and ink must be well protected. Sandwiching each folio within folded sheets of polyester film and then sealing the packages just outside the manuscript edges preserves the folio format while protecting all pages from the air, dust, insects, and handling.

ENVIRONMENTAL REQUIREMENTS

The rarity of the manuscript dictates that storage and exhibition environments give it the maximum protection possible. Deterioration reactions in iron gall ink artifacts are strongly influenced by relative humidity, temperature, light, and air pollution.

Humidity

Because damaging chemical reactions proceed more rapidly in the presence of moisture—even a humid atmosphere—maintaining low humidity is necessary for the preservation of iron gall ink

ENCAPSULATION. Another Washington folio-format manuscript was encapsulated between sheets of archival quality polyester film. Note that the package is sealed just outside the edges of the document; the film does not impregnate the artifact.

objects. Recently, a level below 35 percent has been recommended.[19] This is considerably lower than ambient conditions in many situations and might create damaging repercussions for other nearby artifacts which could require more moisture for physical stability. By storing and exhibiting the "Remarks" in a sealed case, caretakers could more easily maintain a low humidity level while leaving surrounding objects and room conditions unaffected.

To impede the iron ions from mobilizing and to avoid physical stress along repaired split lines, it is important that the low humidity level be constant—around the clock through all seasons of the year.[20] A sealed case, built with conservation quality materials and techniques, can facilitate environmental control.

Temperature

Because higher temperatures accelerate the rate of chemical reactions, maintaining a temperature below 70 degrees F is recommended for both exhibition and storage of paper materials. As with relative humidity, avoiding fluctuations is important, so maintaining a temperature of 68 degrees F (plus or minus three degrees) at all times is advised.

Light

Different materials can withstand different degrees of exposure to light in the visible and ultraviolet ranges. When an object incorporates several materials, the most vulnerable one determines the extent of safe exposure. The "Remarks" paper is robust in this respect, but the ink may be quite vulnerable. Conclusive studies about iron gall inks' resistance to light have not been published, but these inks seem to be more delicate than previously recognized.[21] As a result, conservators recommend that they be exposed to a maximum of 1,115 "footcandle-hours" of visible-range light per year.[22] This limit is calculated by multiplying the number of days a particular sheet is exhibited by the hours per day it is illuminated by the intensity of light hitting its surface, as measured with an incident light meter. This exposure limit assumes that ultraviolet radiation, which damages paper-based artifacts, has been filtered from both natural and artificial light sources and that detectable fading after one hundred years is acceptable. Factoring in an object's rarity and conditions such as pale or chemically unstable ink, a custodian might decide that more limited exposure would be prudent. The beauty of the equation is that the three factors—number of days exhibited, hours per day of display, and intensity of lighting—can be adjusted to create the most desirable balance. For example, if a longer number of exhibition days is important, then the light level and/or daily exhibition period can be reduced. The conventional lighting level for iron gall inks is 5 footcandles, which is significantly dimmer than lighting in offices or public spaces where visible light often measures between 150 and 300 footcandles. Achieving approximately a 98 percent reduction of light level requires effort and planning, but the professional literature offers a vast range of materials and techniques, both simple and sophisticated.

Ultraviolet (UV) radiation is commonly measured in "microwatts per lumen" which indicates its proportion in the visible light falling on an object. Generally, 10 microwatts per lumen is considered the optimum for UV radiation falling on valued objects, while the maximum acceptable amount is 75 microwatts per lumen. These benchmarks are based on the assumption that the amount of visible light is appropriately limited. UV radiation can be filtered from natural and artificial sources by a variety of materials.

Of course the less paper artifacts are exhibited, the less they are subjected to the permanent, cumulative damage that light causes. Once an ink has faded or shifted color, it cannot be regenerated, and paper molecules that have broken cannot be rebuilt.

Air Pollutants

The damage air pollutants cause to artifacts has been recognized since at least the mid-19th century, and as the number and concentration of pollutants increases, protecting valued objects from their action is an ever greater concern. Research indicates that iron gall ink, specifically, is faded by air pollutants and requires protection in both exhibition and storage environments.[23]

Both gaseous and aerosol pollutants (solid materials so tiny they float in the air) are damaging. Gases which are absorbed by paper cause acidification, hydrolysis, and oxidation reactions. The gases are generated from a broad range of sources, most importantly exhausts from industrial plants and automobiles. On a smaller scale, building materials, interior furnishings, electrical equipment, cleaning solvents, and even the artifact itself may generate pollutants. Damage is aggravated in the presence of light and higher relative humidity or temperature levels. Conservation scientists recommend much lower gaseous pollutant levels than those accepted by the U.S. Environmental Protection Agency. To protect valued objects, the following levels are recommended for the three major polluting gases: sulfur dioxide ≤0.35 parts per billion (ppb), nitrogen dioxide ≤2.65 ppb, ozone ≤0.94 ppb, and for carbon dioxide ≤2.50 parts per million (ppm).[24] In addition, there are gases for which numerical thresholds have not been established.

Aerosols abrade surfaces and deposit mold spores, dirt, and oils. If the dust attracts moisture or gases, it can serve as a catalyst for chemical reactions. Particulate pollutants should be filtered to an amount ≤75 micrograms per cubic meter (μg/m3).[25]

Because outside pollutants readily diffuse into buildings, objects should be stored in a progression of rooms, cabinets, and boxes to provide as much tight archival housing as possible. Our limited individual powers to eliminate air pollution emphasize the importance of taking control of the microenvironment around objects: a well-designed exhibition case or housing system can provide a climate very different from the larger environment.

NOTES

1. Fiber analysis by the author, using polarized light microscopy with TAPPI Fibrary references and the red plate test as outlined in Goodway, Martha, "Fiber Identification in Practice," *Journal of the American Institute for Conservation* 26, no. 1 (Spring 1987): 36.

2. Gravell, Thomas and George Miller, *A Catalogue of American Watermarks, 1690–1835*, 1st ed. (New York: Garland Publishing Inc., 1979), xvi.

3. Ibid., image #344. This watermark also appears on stationery that General Washington used to write to Thomas Jefferson on November 9, 1791. The letter belongs to The Library of Congress, General Correspondence of Thomas Jefferson, Box 25, #11619 63–82. See *Gravell Watermarks Database*, <www.ada.cath.vt.edu:591/dbs/gravell>, Record # 35134.

4. Cleveland, Rachel-Ray, "The Ubiquitous Iron Gall Ink: Present Where You May Not Expect to Find It," The History and Treatment of Works in Iron Gall Ink Meeting, Smithsonian Institution, September 12, 2001.

5. Dorning, David, "Iron Gall Inks: Variations on a Theme That Can be Both Ironic and Galling," *The Iron Gall Ink Meeting: Postprints* (Newcastle upon Tyne: University of Northumbria, 2001), 7.

6. Smith, Christine, "So Tasteful: A Note about Iron Gall Ink," in *The Book and Paper Annual*, Vol. 23, (Washington, D.C., 2004).

7. Grant, Julius, *Books & Documents; Dating, Permanence & Preservation* (London: Grafton & Co., 1937), 34; Mitchell, C. Ainsworth, *Inks:*

Their Composition and Manufacture (London: Charles Griffin & Co., 1937), 8.

8. Waters, C. E., *Inks*, National Bureau of Standards Circular C426 (Washington, D.C.: U.S. Government Printing Office, 1940), 3.

9. Gallic acid is the unit upon which tannic acid is built. Tannic acid and gallotannic acid are synonyms.

10. Chase, Philander, Editor in Chief, The Papers of George Washington, Charlottesville, Va.; Martin, James, Orion Analytical, LLC, Williamstown, MA.; and Richards, Gerald, Richards Forensic Services, Laurel, Md. Conversations with the author, July 2003.

11. Banik, Gerhard, "Decay Caused by Iron-Gall Inks," in *Iron-Gall Ink Corrosion: Proceedings of the European Workshop on Iron-Gall Ink Corrosion* (Rotterdam: Museum Boijmans van Beuningen; Amsterdam: Netherlands Institute for Cultural Heritage, 1997), 22.

12. Reissland, Birgit, "Visible Progress of Paper Degradation Caused by Iron Gall Inks," in *The Iron Gall Ink Meeting: Postprints*, 67–71.

13. Iron Gall Ink Test Paper developed by Johan Neevel and Birgit Reissland is available through Preservation Equipment Ltd., Norfolk, England, product #539-3000.

14. The overlays are cited in the catalogue *Printed Books and Manuscripts from the Estate of John F. Fleming*, Christie's Auction House, New York, Sale of November 18, 1988, 175. The adhesive was tested by this author, using the standard iodine-potassium iodide test (e.g., Odegaard, Nancy, Scott Carroll, and Werner Zimmt, *Material Characterization Tests for Objects of Art and Archaeology* [London: Archetype Publications, 2000], 128).

15. Eusman, Elmer and Kees Mensch, "Ink on the Run: Measuring Migration of Iron in Iron Gall Ink," in *The Iron Gall Ink Meeting: Postprints*, 115–122.

16. van Gulik, Robien, "Currently Used Conservation Methods," Iron Gall Ink Corrosion Web Site, <www.knaw.nl/ecpa/ink>, 2; Barrett, Timothy, and Cynthea Mosier, "The Role of Gelatin in Paper Permanence," *Journal of the American Institute for Conservation* 34, no. 3 (Fall/Winter 1995): 173–186.

17. Smith, Christine, "The Last Will and Testament of George Washington: Conservation Treatment Report," prepared for The Circuit Court of Fairfax County, Virginia, April 2003, 30–32.

18. Neevel, Johan, "(Im)possibilities of the Phytate Treatment," in *The Iron Gall Ink Meeting: Postprints*, 125–133. This is only one of many articles that Dr. Neevel has written about the use of calcium phytate to prevent further oxidation of iron gall inks.

19. Banik, Gerhard, "Decay Caused by Iron-Gall Inks," in *Iron-Gall Ink Corrosion: Proceedings of the European Workshop on Iron-Gall Ink Corrosion*, 22; Michalski, Stefan, "Humidity, Temperature, and Pollu-

tion in Libraries and Archives," 1990, unpublished draft cited in Annette Low's "The Conservation of Charles Dickens' Manuscripts" in *The Paper Conservator* 18 (1994): 9.

20. Neevel, J.G., and B. Reissland, "The Ink Corrosion Project at the Netherlands Institute for Cultural Heritage—A Review," *Iron-Gall Ink Corrosion: Proceedings of the European Workshop on Iron-Gall Ink Corrosion,* 39.

21. Reissland, Birgit, and Margaret Cowan, "The Light Sensitivity of Iron Gall Inks," in *Works of Art on Paper: Books, Documents and Photographs: Techniques and Conservation: Contributions to the Baltimore Congress,* eds. Daniels, Vincent et al. (London: International Institute for Conservation, 2002), 183.

22. The intensity of visible-range light is measured in several units, one of which is the footcandle (fc). A footcandle-hour is one hour's exposure to one footcandle of light. Currently accepted guidelines for exhibiting paper artifacts are described in Colby, Karen, "A Suggested Exhibition Policy for Works of Art on Paper," *Journal of the International Institute for Conservation—Canadian Group* 17 (1992).

23. Havermans, John B. G. A., and Nathalie J. M. C. Penders, "The Role of Different Accelerated Ageing Techniques in the Evaluation of Conservation Treatments of Objects Affected with Iron Gall Ink," in *The Iron Gall Ink Meeting: Postprints,* 89–94.

24. *Environmental Control for Museums, Libraries, and Archival Storage Areas,* Technical Brochure 600A, Purafil, Inc., Doraville, Ga., 1993, 1.

25. Ibid.

Burton K. Kummerow
President, Historyworks, Inc.

Historic Sites Appendix 2

MENTIONED IN GEORGE WASHINGTON'S "REMARKS"

A S GEORGE WASHINGTON recalled the events of his youth in his "Remarks" for Colonel David Humphreys, he mentioned several settings that today are interpreted as historic sites. Many have grown into busy urban centers while others are remembered as parks, museums or markers on the side of the road. Traveling from Washington's home base in Virginia, the sites trace his voyages through Maryland into the wilderness backcountry of Pennsylvania.*

VIRGINIA

WILLIAMSBURG—Called by George Washington "*. . . the then seat of Governmt,*" the colonial capital of Virginia was the Commonwealth's political base of operations during the French and Indian War. Washington made the long trip on horseback from the west often to consult with the Governor and General Assembly and to plead for funds and supplies to defend the frontier. Today, Colonial Williamsburg is a world famous restoration and recreation of the 18th-century community so familiar to Washington and his contemporaries.

---

* There are scores of French and Indian War frontier sites between western New York and West Virginia documented and described in detail by Robert B. Swift, *The Mid-Appalachian Frontier: A Guide to Historic Sites of the French and Indian War* (Gettysburg, Pa., 2001).

Contact The Colonial Williamsburg Foundation, P.O. Box 1776, Williamsburg, Virginia 23187 (www.history.org).

ALEXANDRIA—Only eight miles north of Mount Vernon, this port city on the Potomac became George Washington's hometown. It was just five years old at the beginning of the French and Indian War, but Washington referred to it as *"the place of general rendezvous"* for the Virginia troops who marched west to fight the French. In 1755, the new stone Alexandria town-house of John Carlyle became the headquarters for General Edward Braddock as he met with several British royal governors in preparation for his disastrous campaign to capture the Forks of the Ohio.

> *Contact* The Lyceum, built in 1839 as a cultural center, is the home of the Alexandria History Museum, a branch of the Office of Historic Alexandria, 220 N. Washington Street, Alexandria, Virginia 22314. Its website (http://oha.ci.alexandria.va.us) has an online feature entitled "Following in Washington's Footsteps."
>
> The restored John Carlyle House is the Carlyle House Historic Park, Northern Virginia Regional Park Authority, 121 N. Fairfax Street, Alexandria, Virginia 22314 (www.carlylehouse.org).

MOUNT VERNON—The famous Washington family property on the banks of the Potomac River was George Washington's boyhood retreat. After he became the owner of Mount Vernon at the end of the French and Indian War, Washington's forty year love affair with the plantation made it a Virginia showplace.

Today the house and grounds, painstakingly restored by the Mount Vernon Ladies' Association, are are recognized internationally as a center for the study and interpretation of the first president's life and times.

> *Contact* George Washington's Mount Vernon, 3200 George Washington Memorial Parkway, Mount Vernon, Virginia 22121 (www.mountvernon.org)

WINCHESTER—Originally called Fredericktown, the rapidly growing frontier community became a depot and line of defense during the collision between the French and British in the wilderness further west. Washington rode through many times and General Braddock's army stopped here in 1755 to prepare for the rough roads northwest to Fort Cumberland. After Braddock's defeat, the village became Colonel Washington's headquarters at a hastily-built Fort Loudoun, one of a chain of forts raised to protect western Virginia from terrifying French and Indian raids. Washington owned land locally and was elected to his first public office in Winchester, representing Frederick County in the Virginia General Assembly.

> *Contact* George Washington's Headquarters, Braddock and Cork Streets, Winchester, Virginia 22601 (www.winchesteronline.com). The site of Fort Loudoun has been covered by urban development but is interpreted by Colonel Washington's Frontier Forts Association (www.frontierforts.org).

FORT VASS—Vass's (Vause's) Fort was one of a line of twenty-two Virginia strongholds stretching from Fort Cumberland in Maryland to the North Carolina border. It was described as a hundred-foot-square, fifteen-foot-high earthwork and palisade surrounding settler Ephraim Vause's cabin and garrisoned by seventy men. The fortification was attacked and burned by a French and Indian raiding party in 1756 but rebuilt a few months later. It was a vivid memory for George Washington because he *"narrowly escaped"* ambush and certain death nearby while touring the southern forts in the fall of 1756.

> *Contact* The site of Fort Vause, in Shawsville, Montgomery County, was excavated in 1968. The 18th-century settlers' era is interpreted at nearby Virginia's Explore Park, Mile post 115, Blue Ridge Parkway, P.O. Box 8508, Roanoke, Virginia 24014 (www.explorepark.org).

MARYLAND

FORT CUMBERLAND (**Wills Creek**)—This mountain setting, now Cumberland, Maryland, was the gateway to Braddock's Road, the earliest British route to the Forks of the Ohio. George Washington first visited the storehouses of Virginia's Ohio Company, where Wills Creek joins the North Branch of the Potomac River, in 1753. A fort soon followed, christened Fort Cumberland, " . . . *for the purpose of covering the frontiers.*" Here, General Braddock prepared his army for the difficult march west in 1755. Colonel Washington commanded the Virginia troops garrisoned

Appendix 2

HISTORIC SITES
MENTIONED IN
GEORGE
WASHINGTON'S
"REMARKS"

at the fort in the dark days after Braddock's Defeat, engaging in a famous dispute with Captain John Dagworthy, a Maryland officer who claimed he outranked all colonial officers because of his royal commission. The site of Fort Cumberland, on "Fort Hill," was covered by the City of Cumberland, prospering with the presence of the National Road, the Chesapeake & Ohio Canal, and the Baltimore & Ohio Railroad during the 19th century.

Contact The 1850 Gothic Revival Emmanuel Episcopal Church is above much of the fort site. The church interprets the fort with a model and the belowground remains of tunnels as well as a powder magazine; Emmanuel Episcopal Church, 218 Washington Street, Cumberland, Maryland 21502 (www.braddocksmarch.org). Interpretive signs on the church grounds describe the site. A log cabin, purported to be Washington's Headquarters, is at the foot of Fort Hill.

George Washington
REMEMBERS

PENNSYLVANIA

PRESQUE ISLE (Fort de la Rivière au Boeuf)—Twenty-one-year-old George Washington accomplished his remarkable 1753 trek to Presque Isle *"at a most inclement season,"* carrying a message from Virginia to the French to withdraw from the Ohio Valley. He actually traveled only as far as Fort Le Boeuf, a fifteen-mile portage south from Fort de la Presque Isle, which was on the banks of Lake Erie (present Erie, Pennsylvania). The French stockades anchored a reinforced line of advance to claim the Forks of the Ohio, *". . . having descended from Presque Isle* [Erie] *by the Rivers le beouf* (sic) [French Creek] *and Alligany* (sic)." French Creek meets the Allegheny River at Fort Machault or Venango, now Franklin, Pennsylvania.

Contact The site of Fort de la Presque Isle, in downtown Erie, Pennsylvania, is interpreted by the Pennsylvania Historical and Museum Commission at the Erie Maritime Museum, 150 East Front Street, Erie, Pennsylvania 16507 (www.brigniagara.org) and the Erie County Historical Society at the History Center and Cashiers House, 417 State Street, Erie, Pennsylvania 16507 (www.eriehistory.org). The site of Fort Le Boeuf, with a statue of George Washington, is interpreted by the Fort Le Boeuf Historical Society, 31 High Street, Waterford, Pennsylvania 16441 (www.experiencepa. com) and the Edinboro University of Pennsylvania (www.edinboro.edu).

THE FORKS OF THE OHIO—George Washington first noticed and described the Forks when he passed through in late 1753. He later described the Point as "... *the important Post at the conflux of the Alligany* (sic) *and Monangahela* (sic); *with the advantages of which he was forcibly struck.* . . *and earnestly advised the securing of with Militia, or some other temporary force.*" A series of forts occupied the Point during the French and Indian War. The first small English stockade, called **Fort Prince George**, was replaced by **Fort Duquesne** after a large French force overwhelmed the Virginians in early 1754. Fort Duquesne was scuttled in anticipation of its capture by the British four and a half years later. A temporary stockade called **Mercer's Fort** on the banks of the Monongahela River about a thousand feet east of the Point was soon replaced by the giant brick and earth **Fort Pitt**, guaranteeing permanent British control of the Forks. The City of Pittsburgh, one of America's important gateways to the west, grew around the Point and Fort Pitt.

> *Contact* Point State Park now contains an outline defining the site of Fort Duquesne, an original Fort Pitt Blockhouse, the oldest building in western Pennsylvania, administered by the Daughters of the American Revolution and the Pennsylvania Historical and Museum Commission's Fort Pitt Museum in a reconstructed bastion of the fort; Fort Pitt Museum, 101 Commonwealth Place, Point State Park, Pittsburgh, Pennsylvania 15222 (www.fortpittmuseum.com).

FORT NECESSITY—Having lost a race to control the Forks of the Ohio to the French in 1754, Lieutenant Colonel George Washington and his first command were attacked by a large force of French and Indians "... *in a small temporary stockade in the middle of the Intrenchment* (sic) *called Fort necessity erected for the sole purpose its* [the ammunition's] *security, and that of the few stores we had* . . . " Under relentless musket fire from the woods and "... *the most tremendous rain that can be conceived,*" Washington and his badly defeated force surrendered and were allowed to retreat with the honors of war southeast to Wills Creek. The campaign had begun with a clash during which the Virginians and their Indian allies had killed ten members of a French party at nearby Jumonville Glen. The French called it an ambush and an "assassination," using the incident to help start a world war for empire.

Appendix 2

HISTORIC SITES
MENTIONED IN
GEORGE
WASHINGTON'S
"REMARKS"

Contact Fort Necessity, the only national park on a French and Indian War battlefield, is at the Great Meadows, in the Laurel Highlands overlooking the Monongahela River Valley; Fort Necessity National Battlefield, One Washington Parkway, Farmington, Pennsylvania 15437 (www.nps.gov/fone/home.htm/). Two other locations, the Braddock Grave (see below), one and a half miles west of Fort Necessity on U.S. Route 40, and the Jumonville Glen, seven miles northwest, are administered by the United States National Park Service.

THE BRADDOCK ROAD

THE BRADDOCK ROAD—Tracing the hundred-mile-long, twelve-foot-wide 1755 road from its source in Cumberland, Maryland to the banks of the Monongahela River is a challenge on modern roads. General Braddock's " . . . *March through the Mountains & covered Country . . . prepossed* (sic) *. . . in favor of regularity & discipline"* brought *" . . . difficulties to which they were never accustomed in regular Service."* Yet the army, bringing along its heavy artillery and wagons, created a pioneering new road only to suffer one of the greatest defeats in the history of the British Army on July 9, 1755. Just *" . . . 10 miles short of Fort Duquesne,"* the British *" . . . front was attacked; and by the unusual Hallooing and whooping of the enemy, whom they could not see, were so disconcerted and confused, as soon to fall into irretrievable disorder."* General Braddock was mortally wounded and almost all of his officers except George Washington, who was miraculously unhurt, went down. His attack force was destroyed and his equipment and supplies lost.

The defeated British army fell back to a reserve force under the command of Colonel Thomas Dunbar. George Washington, exhausted and *" . . . wholly unfit for the execution of the duty he was sent upon . . . ,"* brought the news of the disaster to Dunbar's Camp after a harrowing all-night ride. Colonel Dunbar almost immediately destroyed most of his equipment and set up "winter quarters" as soon as the survivors marched to Philadelphia in August. General Braddock was *" . . . interred with the honors of war, and it was left to G.W.* [George Washington] *to see this performed . . . they* [his remains] *were deposited in the Road over which the Army, Waggons* (sic) *&ca passed to hide every trace by which the entombment could be discovered."* It would take over three years for British forces to mount another campaign and capture the Forks of the Ohio.

Contact Today, the best place to see the remains of the original Braddock Road is in the area of Fort Necessity.

George Washington
REMEMBERS

Much of the 18th-century road in the Allegheny Mountains is traced by a much straighter U.S. Route 40, the 19th-century National Road. The Battlefield of the Monongahela or Braddock's Defeat has been buried by the boroughs of Braddock and North Braddock and by one of America's oldest steel mills. In spite of the modern industrial landscape, the Monongahela River Valley still retains the dramatic terrain features that existed when the British, French and Indian forces collided. The Braddock's Field Historical Society interprets the battle in America's oldest Carnegie Library (www.einetwork.net/ein/braddock) and owns land that has reclaimed a piece of the battlefield in North Braddock; Braddock's Field Historical Society, 419 Library Street, Braddock, Pennsylvania 15109 (www.museumsusa.org). The site of Dunbar's Camp (near the Jumonville Glen) and the French and Indian War History around the Great Meadows is interpreted by the Braddock Road Preservation Association, 887 Jumonville Road, Hopwood, Pennsylvania 15445 (www.braddockroadpa.org). The Braddock Grave, rediscovered during road building in the early 19th century, is preserved as a unit of the Fort Necessity National Battlefield (see Fort Necessity).

Appendix 2

HISTORIC SITES
MENTIONED IN
GEORGE
WASHINGTON'S
"REMARKS"

THE FORBES ROAD—The year 1758 brought another British effort to capture the Forks of the Ohio, this time cutting a new path from Philadelphia across central Pennsylvania. George Washington, wanting to protect Virginia interests on the Braddock Road, strongly objected to the new route. The large army, commanded by the ailing General John Forbes and his able subordinate Colonel Henry Bouquet, moved deliberately to each fortified stronghold from Philadelphia to Carlisle to Raystown (Fort Bedford). By the fall of 1758, the strike force had conquered most of the rugged mountains and was within forty miles of Fort Duquesne at Loyalhanning (Fort Ligonier). Colonel Washington now led the largest force of provincial troops he commanded before the Revolution. While stationed at Fort Ligonier, he faced the "*. . . circumstance . . . wch involved the life of G.W. in as much jeopardy as it had been before or since . . . G.W. never was in more imminent danger by being between two fires, knocking up with his sword the presented pieces.*" His Virginia troops, separated on a reconnaissance mission, were mistakenly killing each other in the twilight of the day. This "friendly fire" incident, rarely mentioned in any documents, occurred just a few miles west of Fort Ligonier.

Within a few weeks, the British had control of the Forks of the Ohio and Washington's military career was, for the moment, at an end.

Contact The twists and turns of the original 1758 Forbes Road approximately follow what became U.S. Route 30 (part of the east–west transcontinental road called The Lincoln Highway). The source of the road, Philadelphia, has some survivors of the French and Indian War era including the Christ Church, burial place of General John Forbes, and the enduring memory of Benjamin Franklin who played an important role in the early days of the war. A visit to the colonial history of the City of Brotherly Love begins with the Atwater Kent Museum of Philadelphia, 15 South Street, Philadelphia, Pennsylvania 19106 (www.philadelphiahistory. org). A fully reconstructed Fort Ligonier has the most complete interpretation of the 1758 campaign; Fort Ligonier Association, 216 South Market Street, Ligonier, Pennsylvania 15658 (www.fortligonier.org).

George Washington

REMEMBERS

Author Biographies

FRED ANDERSON, *Editor*
Fred Anderson earned his B.A. at Colorado State University and his Ph.D. at Harvard. In addition to articles, essays, and reviews, he has written two books—*A People's Army: Massachusetts Soldiers and Society in the Seven Years' War* (1984) and *Crucible of War: The Seven Years' War and the Fate of Empire in British North America, 1754–1766* (2000). He teaches early American history at the University of Colorado at Boulder.

PHILANDER D. CHASE, *Contributor*
Philander D. Chase has been an editor on the staff of the "Papers of George Washington" for the past thirty years and editor in chief of the project for the past five years.

DON HIGGINBOTHAM, *Contributor*
Don Higginbotham is Dowd Professor of History at the University of North Carolina at Chapel Hill. His books include three volumes on George Washington—*Washington and the American Military Tradition, Washington Reconsidered,* and *Washington: Uniting a Nation.*

BURTON K. KUMMEROW, *Guide to French and Indian War Sites*
Burton K. Kummerow is President of Historyworks, Inc., public history consultants based in Baltimore, Maryland. He brings long experience as an academic historian, a television producer, a museum director, and a writer to his work.

CHRISTINE SMITH, *Conservator*
Christine Smith, President, Conservation of Art on Paper, Inc. (CAPI) in Alexandria, Virginia has treated many Washington manuscripts, including a census of his slaves and his last will and testament. Her work with iron gall ink artifacts has ranged from Italian Renaissance drawings to American fraktur.

MARTIN WEST, *Contributor*
Martin West is the director of Fort Ligonier, a museum and restored/reconstructed British fort, 1758–1766, in southwestern Pennsylvania. He is an adjunct lecturer of history at the University of Pittsburgh and serves on the Advisory Council of George Washington Scholars, Mount Vernon, Virginia.

ROSEMARIE ZAGARRI, *Contributor*
Rosemarie Zagarri is Professor of History at George Mason University. She is the editor of *David Humphreys' "Life of General Washington" with George Washington's "Remarks"* (1991) and the author of *The Politics of Size: Representation in the United States, 1776–1850* (1987) and *A Woman's Dilemma: Mercy Otis Warren and the American Revolution* (1995).

Acknowledgements

THIS publication of George Washington's autobiographical memorandum was made possible by the generous assistance and encouragement of numerous institutions and individuals. Laura Fisher of the Allegheny Conference on Community Development and Lisa Adams of the Garamond Agency provided general coordination of the book.

Martin West would like to acknowledge the inestimable help to the annotation from the staffs of the Papers of George Washington at the University of Virginia, the William L. Clements Library at the University of Michigan, the Darlington Memorial Library at the University of Pittsburgh, St. Vincent College, and, for interlibrary services, the Ligonier Valley Library. Encouragement came from his colleagues at the Braddock's Field Historical Society, Braddock's Road Preservation Society, Bushy Run Battlefield (Pennsylvania Historical and Museum Commission), Fort Necessity National Battlefield (National Park Service), and the Fort Pitt Museum (Pennsylvania Historical and Museum Commission). Indispensable was the aid and support of the board of trustees and staff of Fort Ligonier. Several scholars read and greatly improved the full annotation, including Fred Anderson, Philander D. Chase, Michael N. McConnell and Beverly H. Runge, and specific subject areas were reviewed by René Chartrand, Brian Leigh Dunnigan, Paul E. Kopperman and Burton K. Kummerow. Blanche M. Thomas edited the entire annotation. Penelope West, educator at Fort Ligonier, together with university students Jane West and Benjamin West, assisted with research and electronic formatting.

Fred Anderson would like to thank Don Higginbotham, Rosemarie Zagarri, Martin West, Lisa Adams, and Laura Fisher for their help and kind advice. He also wishes to acknowledge, as ever, Virginia DeJohn Anderson and Samuel DeJohn Anderson, whose contributions go well beyond anything they might imagine, or he could describe.

Philander D. Chase would like to acknowledge the work of Associate Editor Beverly H. Runge in checking and perfecting the document text, which, of course, is the basis on which everything else is built.

Don Higginbotham would like to acknowledge the assistance of Peter R. Henriques and Kathy Higginbotham.

Rosemarie Zagarri would like to thank Fred Anderson, Peter R. Henriques, and Don Higginbotham for helpful advice and assistance in preparing her contribution. She also acknowledges the University of Georgia Press for permission to use selected material from the introduction to *David Humphrey's "Life of General Washington," with George Washington's Remarks*, edited by Rosemarie Zagarri, © 1991 by the University of Georgia Press.

George Washington

REMEMBERS

Index

George Washington

R E M E M B E R S

Index